THE SMALL-BOAT
SAILOR'S BIBLE

A ketch homeward bound in the late-afternoon sun. (Photo by Bob Luckey, courtesy Newsday, *Long Island*)

THE SMALL-BOAT SAILOR'S BIBLE

By
Hervey Garrett Smith

Revised by Theodore A. Jones

DOUBLEDAY & COMPANY, INC.
GARDEN CITY, NEW YORK

To
HOWARD NIXON, JR.,
who shows every promise of becoming a fine sailor.
Which would please his grandfather greatly.

ISBN: 0-385-05527-7
Library of Congress Catalog Card Number 73—82247
Copyright © 1964, 1974 by Hervey Garrett Smith
Printed in the United States of America

CONTENTS

THE SMALL-BOAT
SAILOR'S BIBLE

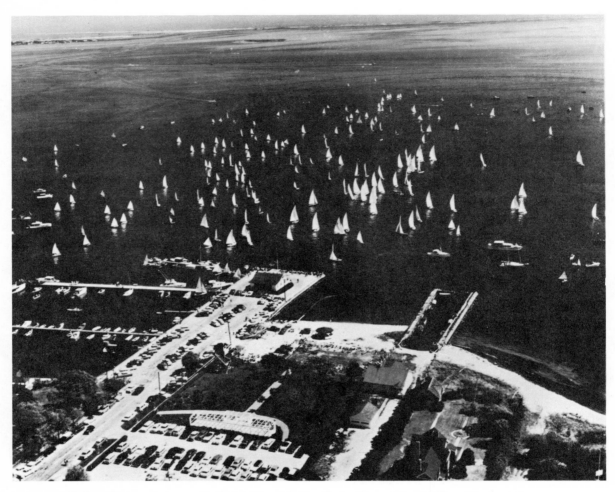

Labor Day regatta at Bellport Bay Yacht Club, Long Island, New York. (Courtesy Brookhaven Industrial Development Committee and Robert B. Lea)

Chapter 1

CHOOSING YOUR FIRST BOAT

The purpose of this book is to aid you in getting the full measure of enjoyment that may be had through owning a sailboat and going to sea for pleasure.

How well you succeed will depend to a large extent on your getting started right.

There are a number of important factors that must be carefully considered before you can reach an intelligent decision in choosing your first boat. If you are a novice, your judgment obviously cannot be based on your own experience. But you *can* profit by the mistakes of others.

One thing should be understood at the start. The size of your boat or pocketbook has very little bearing on your *enjoyment* of sailing. You can have just as much fun exploring the creek or cove in your home port in an 8-foot sailing pram, as you can cruising for a weekend in a 40-foot auxiliary. The difference is not in degree, but in kind. Even if your initial investment must be a very modest one, the main thing is to get out there and *sail,* and it matters little if you get no more than a couple of miles from your mooring during your first season. It all adds up to experience, and the more you get the more fun you'll have.

Before you start looking at boats you should have a clear idea of what you're looking for. This means making a careful analysis of your requirements, and the conditions your boat must meet. Once you have assembled all the facts, you'll have a pretty fair picture of the type of boat that best suits your needs.

Intended Use

Do you want a day sailer, a racer, or a cruising sailboat? A boat is a compromise, designed with a particular use in mind.

The day sailer is what its name implies—a boat in which several people can enjoy a day's relaxed sailing, with reasonable comfort. It is easy to sail, easy to maintain, and relatively inexpensive. Its size will generally be under 20 feet.

The racing boat is designed for competition and strenuous sailing, not for comfort. Its handling calls for more competence and experience than the day sailer, and its maintenance is more time-consuming and expensive. Since it is designed as an efficient, high-performance machine, sails, rigging, and gear are much more complicated.

You'll find certain types of small boats that can be used for both day sailing and racing. Day sailers, in some localities, are used for organized class racing, and a few racing types are quite practical for day sailing. For example, the 19-foot *Lightning* is an international racing-class boat which furnishes keen competition everywhere. But because it has a large cockpit, has a high initial stability, and is easy to handle, it also makes an excellent day sailer. Thus, a boat of this type has greater utility than many.

The cruising sailboat, since it has living accommodations and auxiliary power, either inboard or outboard, is a mobile home afloat. You don't have to head for home at sundown, as in a day sailer. You can wander where you will, explore strange waters, and stay out for a weekend or a month's vacation. But the cruising sailboat is not generally considered suitable for the novice's first boat. It demands a lot of sailing experience, a high degree of seamanship, and a working knowledge of many different arts and skills.

What kind of boat, and for how many people? This half-century-old catboat holds eighteen with ease—but not when the journey is long or the sea rough. (Photo by Macklin Boettger)

For How Many People?

One of the prime causes of boating accidents is overloading. Every boat has a designed load capacity well within the limits of safety. If you are contemplating a boat that was designed to be sailed with three people aboard, don't invite four friends to go sailing with you. It would be poor seamanship. Decide how many your boat can accommodate safely. If you are married and have a couple of small fry, choose a boat with a fair-sized cockpit and a comfortable place to sit, a boat that is easy to handle and that sails on its bottom, and doesn't require a family of acrobats to keep it right side up.

Nature of the Waters in Which You'll Be Sailing

Choosing a boat will be a lot simpler if you first familiarize yourself with conditions in your local waters. What facilities are there for launching your boat? Where can you rent dock space, and for how much? Learn the controlling depth of the water, the amount of rise and fall of tides, navigational hazards, if any, and the direction and strength of prevailing winds.

The best way to learn these things is to *ask lots of questions* of local skippers. They can tell you what types of boat are suitable for the local waters, and why. They know the trials that beset the newcomer, and they are usually happy to talk boats with an interested listener.

Maintenance

All boats require maintenance. Someone must care for them, repair minor damage, and combat the wear and tear that occur in normal use. Most boatowners have as much fun working on their boats as they do sailing them. If you are handy with tools, you can keep maintenance costs to a minimum; if you are not, you'll have to pay someone to do the work for you. Boatyard labor currently runs up to $10.00 per hour. Hauling and storing your boat in a boatyard will cost a minimum of $8.00 per foot of length.

If you plan to keep your boat in the water, you'll have to rent a mooring or dock space. Marinas, either community or privately owned, rent slips on a fixed basis, depending on over-all length of the boat. While "average" costs are hard to determine, community-owned slips generally run about $50 to $150 per season. Private marinas are considerably higher, since they maintain numerous shore facilities, such as water supply and electricity, ice, sanitary facilities, showers, and laundromats.

You can eliminate these expenses and reduce maintenance costs to an absolute minimum by trailerboating. Trailer your boat to whatever body of water you wish to explore, and bring it home when you are through sailing. Park it in your own back yard, where you can keep an eye on it and fuss with it whenever you like. No docking or mooring fees, no wondering how it's faring while you are away. Most waterfront communities maintain public launching ramps for residents, either free or with a permit costing about $2.00. With your boat in or next to your garage, you can do your own work at your own convenience. You can think of maintenance costs in terms of the price of a couple of cans of paint, varnish, brushes, and sandpaper.

You can readily understand why trailering is a big factor in the tremendous growth of popular boating. We discuss trailering in detail in Chapter 24.

Resale Values

A most important consideration in buying a boat is its resale value, because the novice's first boat is invariably traded in for another after the first or second season. By that time he is no longer a novice. He has had enough experience to judge a boat more accurately, and he knows what he wants in a boat.

If his boat was a type currently popular in his locality, and he had given it excellent care, he would have no difficulty in selling it for 30 to 35 percent less than its original cost. It is a case of owning a type for which there is a continuing demand.

But if his boat was an "orphan," the only one of its kind in the area, and perhaps not even suitable for the local waters, he might have a hard time disposing of it at any price—unless, of course, he finds another novice less informed than himself.

Many years ago, when a dollar consisted of one hundred pennies, I built an 18-foot combination day sailer and racer, at a total cost of $475. For fifteen enjoyable years I sailed and raced it, fair weather and foul. Then, one day, $700 was waved in my face . . . and the new owner sailed it away, happy as a clam at high water. After three years it was again exchanged, and this time the settlement was $900. Eighteen years of fun for two families, with a profit!

The moral of this story is that you can get a handsome return on your investment if you have a boat that is in demand, and give it the loving care it deserves.

Chapter 2

NEW OR USED BOAT?

The question of whether to buy a new boat or a used one generally hinges upon two things: how much you are prepared to spend, and what you can buy at that price. Unfortunately, the boat that seems best suited to your needs frequently costs more than your budget allows, and in that predicament, the only answer is compromise.

Let's suppose that $1,500 is the absolute limit you can afford to spend. You have a wife and two youngsters and want a day sailer for the whole family to enjoy. After making the rounds of the dealers, you find an 18-footer that is exactly suited to your requirements, but to your dismay the new-boat price is $2,000 complete with sails. So you lower your sights a bit, and find a smart little 16-footer that sells for $1,495 new. Because it fits your pocketbook, you are tempted to buy it. But it *doesn't* fit your *needs,* and right here is the place for some earnest consideration.

The 16-footer may well be a very fine boat, and well worth the money, but with two adults and two children aboard she would be cramped, unhandy, an indifferent sailer, and under certain conditions, unsafe.

You'd best be advised to go back to the 18-footer of your first choice and look for a *used* one, and it is reasonable to expect that you could find one in good condition for $1,500. To be sure, she may have a couple of gouges in her topsides, her mahogany seats and coamings may be dingy and devoid of varnish, and her frayed sheets may resemble discarded clotheslines. But if she is basically sound, these are of minor importance. You would be safer, more comfortable and carefree, and have more enjoyment with her than with the pretty little 16-footer.

If you are a novice, and the boat of your choice is priced within your budget, it is wise to buy a *new* boat. You'll then be assured of carefree sailing, and fun without worry, knowing with certainty that your boat and all its gear is in perfect condition.

A new boat will require a minimum amount of maintenance, and you can keep that "new" look for several seasons, which will greatly enhance the resale value. There is also the thrill of getting the first use of it, with no worries about repairs or replacements in the immediate future.

Buying a used boat is a different story. On the one hand it is fraught with danger. On the other, there is the possibility of more boat for less money, improving your investment while enjoying it, and eventually selling it at a profit, which in turn can lead to a bigger or better boat.

One piece of advice deserves the greatest possible emphasis. Unless you have had considerable experience, and know a lot about boats, don't ever buy a used boat without getting an opinion from a disinterested expert. What you want from him is an analysis of the exact condition of the boat you are considering. Is there any sign of dry rot, bad fastenings, broken frames, fractured fiberglass, or previous damage? What repairs or replacements are needed, if any, and what they would cost in time and money? Is there a complete inventory of sails and gear, and what is its condition? Finally, what, if anything, does he know of the past history of that particular boat?

Armed with this information, you are in a position to bargain wisely, and to judge whether the boat is worth the asking price.

What to Look For in a Used Wood Boat

The most important thing to look for in a used boat is the condition of the hull. By that we mean the soundness of the structure, *not* the finish. After all, "finish" is superficial, nothing more than paint and varnish. A coat of paint can hide a lot of bad news, and it's what's underneath that counts. The novice is invariably influenced by a boat's eye-appeal, the shiny chromed hardware, the gay and colorful cockpit cushions, and the sparkling paint job. But he fails to see the punky wood in the corner of the transom, the cracked frames, the gaping garboard seams, and the plank where the fastenings are holding absolutely nothing.

For a thorough inspection of a used boat, it must be out of the water, on dry land, where you can get under it to examine the bottom. Every square inch of bottom planking should be checked. Look for signs of a split plank. Go over all the seams and see if they are fairly tight. If one plank stands away from its neighbor, particularly where they butt together, it is invariably a sign that fastenings have let go. The garboard seams, along the keel, are a common source of trouble in older boats. If they are over a quarter of an inch wide, beware. It can be an indication that something is wrong inside, such as rotten frames, bad fastenings, or both. Probing with a penknife often locates trouble. Calking should be firm . . . if the knife blade shows it to have the consistency of mud, recalking will be needed.

Dry rot is not always visible, and often is unsuspected. It is a fungus, whose spores thrive and develop through a combination of heat and dampness, often caused by lack of ventilation. Much of it is caused by rainwater working down between two members, where it is trapped and cannot evaporate. Two common ways of locating rot are by sound and by feel. If you tap a plank with something solid, like a screwdriver handle, it will make a hard, sharp sound. If you tap where rot is present, it will sound soft, as though you were striking cork. Probing sound wood with a penknife, you'll meet with resistance. Where there is rot the blade will go into the wood as though it were cheese.

If a boat has been out of water for several years, it may not be a bargain at any price. Boats are meant to be in the water. A couple of years of exposure to sun and wind dries out the wood excessively. Severe checkering occurs, particularly in oak, and the abnormal shrinking of the planking puts great strains on the fastenings. To put such a boat in serviceable condition can be a costly operation, and it will never be as good as it was before the elements pulled it apart.

Do you want a new boat or used? With careful maintenance a boat will last a life-time. If you plan to buy a used boat, check it over carefully out of the water.
(*Photo by Theodore A. Jones*)

If you are investing several thousands of dollars in a used boat, you should seek professional advice. For a small fee, a marine surveyor will make a detailed, careful inspection, and deliver a complete report of the boat's condition. He will not try to "sell" you, and you'll get an expert, unbiased opinion that can save you more than the amount of his fee.

What to Look For in a Used Fiberglass or Aluminum Boat

Although fiberglass and aluminum boats do not deteriorate in the same ways as wood boats, they are subject to damage and subtle but potentially serious defects. Many of the old-time surveyors, used to wood construction, will not survey fiberglass or aluminum boats. If you cannot find someone who is knowledgeable, you will have to do it yourself.

Things to look for in fiberglass are cracks or crazes in the exterior gel coat. These can indicate either a severe collision—with possible unseen structural damage—or improper chemical mix of the resin when the boat was built. Since fiberglass boats are easily repaired, the latter problem is probably the more serious as it will mean refinishing the entire hull. Shining a strong light through the laminate (if it is unpainted) will show up cracks and strains that may not appear on the surface. These may not be serious if they are small and there aren't many, but a radial pattern of cracks or crazes will indicate a severe blow that has weakened the laminate.

Dull gel coat, dirty bilges and corroded fittings are not serious defects in themselves, but they indicate that the boat has not had the best of care. It is likely that the new owner of such a boat will be plagued by minor breakdowns that could occur at dangerous times. It will also take a considerable amount of work to restore such a boat to its original beauty.

Aluminum boats are subject to corrosion, particularly in salt water, which should not be serious if the proper alloy has been used. The only way to identify the alloy is to refer to the builder's original specifications. Aluminum oxide, a white, powder-like substance, forms a protective coating on the metal which, in the proper alloys, inhibits further corrosion. Aluminum should be painted, however, and if the painted surface is smooth and uniform, the metal underneath should be in good condition. Watch out for cracks in the finish which could be signs of damage or serious corrosion. A pitted surface may indicate the presence of electrolitic corrosion which could be very serious if the electrolysis has been prolonged and widespread.

No boat is perfect, and many good buys may be found among boats that need work. If you are not experienced in the type of repairs that are needed, consult a reputable boatyard or craftsman who is, and ask for an estimate of the cost of repairs. Deduct this cost from the fair market value of the boat. A large hole in a fiberglass hull may appear to be a mortal wound, but a fiberglass expert might be able to make a "good as new" repair, quite undetectable to anyone but a qualified expert, for as little as $50 or $100. If the purchase price is right (it likely will be— if the seller knew how simple the repair was, he'd take care of it himself and get a better price for the boat), such a boat can be a very good buy.

In one sense a used boat is a challenge. If the boat is structurally sound, you have an opportunity to improve your investment. Before and after the sailing season, you can have a lot of fun giving it a complete face-lifting. The open seams, the dents and scars of previous years can be obliterated. The high spots in the planking, the alligatored paint on the deck, and the peeling varnish on the coamings, all respond to the judicious use of paint remover, sandpaper, and elbow grease. It will keep you busy for many hours, but it's your own time, and when you're working on a boat you love, your time isn't worth a cent.

Chapter 3

WOOD, FIBERGLASS, OR ALUMINUM?

Of these three boat-building materials, no one can be called "best." The inherent characteristics of each differ from the others, and each requires different structural design and fabricating techniques. You can have a boat that is strong, seaworthy, and good-looking whether it is built of one or the other, so your choice is largely a matter of personal preference. Your best bet is to get the opinions of experienced boatowners in each category, and compare the respective merits and shortcomings of the materials.

Wood

The best argument in favor of wood boats is that they have been in use for over four thousand years. They have been tested and proved down through the ages in nature's own laboratory, the seven seas. Despite the scientific and technological discoveries of recent decades, man has not been able to produce a substitute having all the natural qualities of wood.

By virtue of all those years of experience, we have learned about all there is to know concerning wood, and can accurately predict its performance. We know its natural enemies and how to combat them. We know its life expectancy and how to insure its fulfillment. A boat of wood that has been well built, and has had proper maintenance, can have a much longer useful life than its owner. Repairs and alterations can be done easily. All that is required is simple, common tools and simple skills, and materials readily obtained anywhere. Maintenance presents no serious problems, is within the ability of almost anyone, and generally involves nothing more than the judicious use of sandpaper, paint, and varnish.

Earlier we mentioned the susceptibility of wood boats to dry rot. Fortunately, wood preservatives have been developed that effectively prevent the fungus from getting a foothold, or that kill it where it has started its dirty work. In the better class of boats, all members are liberally dosed with preservative at the time of building.

There are four types of construction employed in building wood boats. First, there is the oldest and commonest type, the framed and planked hull with calked seams. This makes a boat that is strong and flexible, with the ability to wring and twist under stress, and yet recover. The principal criticism one hears of the planked boat is that the seams are sometimes a source of annoying leaks. The answer to this, of course, is proper maintenance and constant vigilance.

Plywood

The advent of waterproof plywood led to a second type of construction, which eliminated the calked seams, made a smoother finishing surface, and resulted in a stronger, stiffer hull. Unfortunately, plywood sheets cannot be bent to a compound curve, and the boat is limited in design to a flat or V-bottom, with hard chines.

The principal disadvantage of plywood planking is its tendency to delaminate if the edges are not properly sealed. Since the grain of the wood in each layer of veneer runs at right angles to that of its neighbors, tremendous stresses are set up when water gets in and the fibers swell. In the better class of boats, all edges are sealed and bedded with waterproof glue or bedding compound.

Naturally, some sailors do not like V-bottom hulls, but prefer the traditional round bottom with developed sections. This preference has led to a third type of construction, the molded-plywood hull. Instead of flat, prefabricated sheets of plywood, the veneers are laminated over a mandrel, or mold, having the curved sections. The result is a great improvement over the V-bottom, or hard-chine boat. The one-piece molded shell has such great strength and rigidity that ribs or frames are unnecessary, and the interior is smooth, clean, and free of obstructions. Maintenance is easier and simpler than with any other type, for there are no seams to give trouble, and the use of waterproof glue eliminates many of the metal fastenings required in other types of construction. As an added bonus, the absence of

frames and fastenings means a very substantial saving in weight.

Lastly, there is the strip-built type of construction. Here the planking is in the form of nearly square, narrow strips, edge-nailed and glued to each other with waterproof glue. Instead of ribs or frames, a few structural bulkheads give the necessary support. As in the molded plywood type, you have, in effect, a one-piece hull of great strength, no calked seams to leak, and a smooth interior. Currently, it is used mainly in the building of cruising auxiliaries.

Fiberglass

The production of fiberglass boats has increased tremendously in the past few years, primarily because the material lends itself to mass production methods. Originally, fiberglass was confined mainly to small outboard-powered boats, but now the large majority of sailing craft, from small day sailers to large cruising auxiliaries, are fiberglass. Instead of having the many fitted parts and hundreds of fastenings employed in building with wood, the fiberglass hull can be molded in one piece, deck and cabin trunk and interior structures may also be single units, and the number of man-hours required to build a boat are greatly reduced.

The combination of plastic resins and glass fibers produces a "critical" material. It requires a high degree of technical knowledge and skill on the part of the builder, much specialized equipment, and strict control of every step to build a fiberglass boat of high quality. Therefore, in buying a fiberglass boat, compare the reputation and experience of the builders, not the price.

The main advantages of fiberglass boats

The Thunderbird may be bought in fiberglass or may be home built of plywood.
This is a small cruising boat that also races as a one-design fleet in some areas.
(Photo courtesy Mass. Bay Thunderbird Assn.)

are their one-piece construction, absence of seams, and freedom from leaks, both above and below deck. Seats, tanks, ice-boxes, berths, and other interior units can be molded in place, forming an integral part of the hull. In small craft, air compartments or flotation material are molded in as part of the unit, and the boat is nearly unsinkable. In larger boats, even the ballast can be permanently sealed within the structure.

On the debit side, fiberglass has some inherent characteristics that are not so desirable. The material is hard, dense, and stable. By stable, I mean that it neither shrinks nor expands with changing temperature or humidity. On the other hand, it has practically no elasticity. This means that when subjected to a sharp blow, it generally fractures, instead of flexing with the impact and recovering. The metal automobile body will be dented from a blow without fracturing the metal, but a fiberglass hull will not dent . . . either it will resist the blow or it will fracture. In the better-built boats this is recognized and taken care of by "beefing up," or increasing the wall thickness in all vulnerable areas.

Repairing a fiberglass boat is easy. Repair kits, complete with instructions, are obtainable for minor injuries that are within the scope of the amateur's abilities. A boat with a two-foot hole in the topside requires a lot more technical knowledge and skill than most amateurs possess, but can be repaired quickly and often inexpensively.

The slick, highly polished appearance of fiberglass boats resembles the finish of automobile bodies. The surface is generally obtained by a 10- to 20-mil-thick gel coat of pigmented resin that is bonded to the hull in the molding process. Since this coating is extremely thin, it is easily damaged by the scraping and banging that a boat gets in normal use. In restoring the finish of these scratches or surface abrasions, it is usually possible to match the original finish of the surrounding areas.

It would appear that the normal life of the original finish is over five years, depending on how fussy you are about appearance. Maintenance of the finish is much akin to the care of your car, requiring regular cleaning, waxing, and buffing. Refinishing means painting the whole boat, preferably with an epoxy type of marine paint. The application of anti-fouling bottom paints to fiberglass has given trouble in some instances, in that it is often difficult to obtain a good bond. Special primers have been developed, and specific procedures have been found most successful. Needless to say, the manufacturers' step-by-step instructions should be followed to the letter.

Aluminum

The manufacture of aluminum boats got its real start after World War II. There was plenty of surplus aluminum, and fabricating methods had been developed in the aircraft industry. Unfortunately, aircraft aluminum of that period was not compatible with salt water, and those early boats promptly corroded, popped their rivets, and had a very short life. Aluminum boats got a bad name and as a result the aluminum producers developed new alloys to eliminate completely the possibility of salt-water corrosion.

The new alloys can be immersed in sea water for several years, without any protective coating, and there will be no noticeable corrosive effects. Builders of aluminum boats today are using these alloys, with greatly improved building techniques.

A highly skilled method of welding has replaced riveting, resulting in a hull of exceptional strength and rigidity.

In some respects, boats of aluminum are superior to those of wood or fiberglass. First of all, they are far less subject to critical structural damage. Severe shock can dent or crumple the hull without fracturing the metal. Therefore there is less danger of springing a leak as a result of grounding or collision.

Along with high strength, a slight saving in weight is obtained through building with aluminum. In the case of cruising auxiliaries, this saving can be utilized for larger tank capacity, more refrigeration, more equipment, and resultant increased cruising range.

Surface finishes stand up longer than on wood, and maintenance is simple and infrequent.

While there are a few sailing dinghies and day sailers available, the use of aluminum in sailing craft is found mainly in the larger, custom-built cruising auxiliaries.

The disadvantages of aluminum boats are their relatively high initial cost and the problem of repairs and alterations. Very few boatyards are experienced in the specialized techniques required in working with marine aluminum.

Chapter 4

KIT BOATS

"Do-it-yourself" kit boats have great appeal to the novice who wants to get into sailing with the least investment. They can be had for almost any type of boat, from a small sailing pram dinghy to a sizable cruising auxiliary, and in various stages of completion. Savings of 50 percent or more in cost are possible, depending, of course, upon the amateur's abilities and his experience with boats.

The simplest kits are the most difficult to assemble a boat from, since they consist generally of framing components and templates or patterns, and little else. You are furnished the stem, transom, knees, frames, and perhaps a building jig for setting up. Templates for planking, decking, and other parts are supplied, but you'll have to obtain the materials and fastenings locally. Sails, spars, rigging, and hardware are not included. Kits such as these are not recommended for the novice.

The "pre-cut" kit is more complete. It consists of finished frames, planking, trim, and all other members cut fairly close to size, and fastenings and hardware. Some beveling, trimming, and fitting will be required, and simple hand tools will suffice.

The prefabricated kit goes a step further. Practically all parts are finished, and have been fitted. All you have to do is assemble and fasten them together, install hardware, then sand and paint. A kit of this type invariably includes spars, rigging, and sails.

Some builders also supply a bare shell. This is a completed hull, without trim, floorboards, seats or other interior details. The work required to finish the boat is relatively easy and not of a critical nature.

So you have a wide variety of boats to choose from, and you can pick the kit that lies within your ability. For a modest cash outlay, and considerable time and effort, you can have a boat of your own building that can give you many happy hours of sailing. There is one serious objection to kit boats, and you should give it sober thought before plunging headlong. These boats invariably have a very low resale value. Few amateurs have the experience, skill, and equipment to build a boat of professional quality. Poor joinery, improper fastenings, and numerous mistakes may sometimes be concealed by a fancy paint job, but a season's wear and tear generally reveals a boat's amateur origin. The boat might perform well, and give much enjoyment to its builder, but if its workmanship is substandard it hasn't much of a chance against professional competition in the used-boat market.

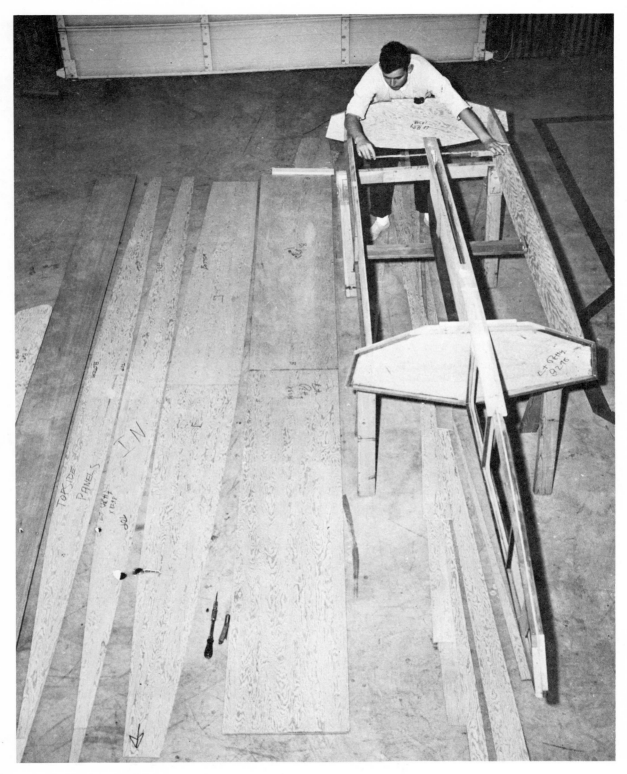

Building an International Fireball from a kit. (Photo by Sgt. F. Cannatta)

If you are considering a kit boat designed and intended for racing, skilled workmanship becomes imperative. All one-design racing classes have strict rules and requirements, such as minimum weights, various measurements, and controlled tolerances. Unless a boat meets these restrictions, and is certified by the official class measurer, it will not be allowed to race. To build a boat within these limits that can compete successfully against boats built by professionals, requires expert craftsmanship.

Chapter 5

THE DAY SAILER

In its original concept, the day sailer was a small boat, generally a centerboarder, with a large open cockpit and a simple rig of jib and mainsail designed for easy, relaxed sailing. It was essentially a family boat of great utility, in which six or eight people could while away the daylight hours on the water. You could sail to a beach for a picnic, anchor awhile for a swim, or try your luck at fishing, and at least once during the season you could take a never-to-be-forgotten evening sail under the light of a full moon. There was no protection from the elements—when it rained you got wet, and under a hot sun you broiled—and at sundown you headed home.

But in recent years the simple day sailer described has been developed far beyond the original concept, and you may now have a day sailer-racer, a day sailer-over-nighter, and even a day sailer-racer-cruiser. Its utility has been expanded to include about every activity you could desire.

Many a youngster has "cruised" in his day sailer, with a tent-fly over the boom and a sleeping bag on the floorboards. But now you can get a day sailer with a small cuddy, or shelter cabin, a settee berth on port and starboard sides, and a cockpit awning with side curtains that convert the entire cockpit into one big cabin. Clamp a small outboard motor on a stern bracket and you have a midget cruising auxiliary.

DAY SAILER. *Fiberglass; length over all, 16 feet, 9 inches; waterline, 16 feet; beam, 6 feet, 3 inches; weight, 580 pounds. Trailable. The cockpit will accommodate six to eight. (Courtesy The O'Day Corporation)*

Chapter 6

THE RACING SAILBOAT

Probably no sport in the world requires such a wide variety of specialized skills as yacht racing. In varying degrees, you'll need a working knowledge of meteorology, tides and currents, racing rules, offensive and defensive tactics, sail handling, boat tuning, and maintenance.

No other sport demands such a high degree of sportsmanship. Once you are over the starting line and beyond the visual range of the race committee, you are strictly on your honor to respect the racing rules and voluntarily report any infraction.

But the most important aspect of racing is the reward, and we don't mean the silver trophy for the winner. Racing teaches you good seamanship in the shortest possible time, sharpens your skills, and promotes self-discipline. An inexperienced sailor will learn more in one race than he would in half a dozen afternoons of loafing along by himself.

A number of requirements must be carefully considered before you buy a racing boat. First, find out whether there is an active, organized class in your locality. Next, be sure that the boat of your choice meets the class rules. It should be officially measured and registered with the class. In return, you'll be awarded a certificate as evidence that your boat is eligible.

Yacht club affiliation is practically a necessity. It is the yacht clubs that organize and run the races and provide your competition. Membership in a recognized club or class association entitles you to participation in interclub races, as well as sectional, national, and international meets.

One other important requirement is a dependable crew. Racing demands a high order of teamwork, and no skipper can expect much teamwork with a strange crew. You'll need a crew that has the time and the interest to sail with you not only in every race, but during many hours of practice. Working together to get the highest possible performance out of the boat, the crew gets to know the skipper's every whim and can anticipate his moves. The skipper can concentrate on his sailing without the distracting necessity of explaining how and why he wants the sails trimmed.

Be sure you have a crew lined up that will stick with you all season, win or lose, fair weather and foul.

One-Design Classes

To list and describe all the active racing types in these pages would be impractical;

it would take a sizable book to cover the field adequately. We can, however, break them up into categories of a sort, and learn their characteristics.

To begin with, the majority of racing boats under 24 feet are centerboarders; they can be easily carried on a trailer, launched from the beach, and sailed in shoal waters. Hull shapes will vary among flat, V, and round bottoms and may be made of sheet plywood, molded plywood, or fiberglass. Many of the newer classes have built-in flotation, in one form or another, and the boats will float if capsized.

Most topflight racing skippers come from the ranks of the juniors. Youngsters from twelve to eighteen get their basic training in small boats through junior racing, generally under the supervision of experienced instructors. With maturity, and a background of several years' experience, they advance to larger boats and adult competition. The one-design classes favored for junior racing will, naturally, vary with the locality. Therefore, you'll find some classes restricted to a limited area, others organized on a national scale, and a few international.

BLUE JAY. *Length over all, 13 feet, 6 inches; waterline, 11 feet, 5 inches; beam, 5 feet, 2 inches; weight, 275 pounds. Trailable. Racing crew, maximum of three.* (*Courtesy McKean Boats*)

There are several catalogs and annual periodicals that list sailboat classes currently available.

BLUE JAY

The Blue Jay has become one of the most popular classes of small boats for basic training and junior racing. There are, currently, more than five thousand registered owners, and ninety-three fleets, in the United States and Canada. It measures 13 feet, 6 inches over all, has an arc bottom, and was originally built of marine plywood although most Blue Jays are now built of fiberglass. The sail area of jib and mainsail is 90 square feet, and it carries a spinnaker. Prices start about $1,700 for a completed boat with sails, and it is available in kit form, in various stages of completion.

Although it is designed primarily for youngsters, in some areas adults race in them, and the clubs now have two divisions—junior and senior.

SNIPE

The International Snipe Class is one of the largest one-design racing classes in the world, and one of the oldest. More than twenty thousand boats have been built in the last forty years, and there are active racing fleets in twenty-eight countries.

Designed by the late William F. Crosby, these 15½-foot, V-bottom sloops have a sail area of 128 square feet in jib and mainsail. The early Snipe had a planked hull, and carried a small working jib, but it now has a Genoa jib, and the hull construction may be plank, plywood, or fiberglass. New boats cost from $1,650 to $1,800, and kits may be had from $500 up.

The Snipe is a lively fast boat, a smart sailer, and very sensitive to handle. Whether you are fourteen or forty, it offers sharp competition and plenty of thrills.

LIGHTNING

With twelve thousand registered boats in over three hundred fleets, the Lightning is one of America's leading one-design classes. It is very popular with juniors who want a larger boat, a "next step up" toward senior competition. Many clubs have adopted the Lightning for junior racing and instruction.

A 19-footer, it has a fiberglass hull with an arc bottom (originally designed for wood construction), has 177 square feet of sail area, and carries a spinnaker. New boats cost $4,000.

With its large, roomy cockpit, the whole family can use the Lightning for day sailing. It has good initial stability and is easy to handle.

SOLING

One of the most popular keelboats is the Olympic Soling, which was designed by Norwegian Jan Linge in 1966 and won selection as an International Class in 1968. The Soling is 26 feet, 9 inches over all; has a beam of 6 feet, 3 inches; displaces 2,200 pounds, of which 1,275 is a cast-iron keel, and carries 233 square feet of sail. Hull construction is fiberglass.

In spite of its heavy keel and three-man crew, the Soling is an exciting and sophisticated racing machine. Because of its Olympic status, the Soling has many active racing fleets throughout the world. This is a rapidly expanding class with well over 3,000 boats world wide. Cost is over $5,000.

SNIPE. *Molded fiberglass, wood planking, or plywood-covered fiberglass; length over all, 15 feet, 6 inches; waterline, 13 feet, 6 inches; beam, 5 feet; weight, 440 pounds. Trailable. Racing crew, two. (Courtesy Gerber's Boat Works)*

LIGHTNING. *Length over all, 19 feet; waterline, 15 feet, 10 inches; beam, 6 feet, 6 inches; weight, 700 pounds. Trailable. Racing crew, three. (Photo by Peter Barlow)*

Solings from Canada and Bermuda racing in Bermuda Week Regatta. (Courtesy Bermuda News Bureau)

OPTIMIST PRAM

Just after World War II, the Optimist Club of Clearwater, Florida, was looking for a small, inexpensive boat that youngsters could use as a training boat. Clark Mills, a local boatbuilder, designed and built the first Optimist Pram in one weekend, and now there are over 20,000 racing throughout the world.

The Optimist Pram is exclusively a junior boat. It measures 7 feet, 8 inches over all, weighs 60 pounds, and carries 35 square feet of sail. It is intended to be built of plywood, with many thousands having been home-built, but is also available in fiberglass. The Optimist Pram represents an absolute minimum racing yacht both in size and cost.

Optimist Prams are an ideal junior boat, being inexpensive, easy to build, yet fun to sail. (Courtesy Miami-Metro Dept. of Publicity and Tourism)

High-Performance Sailboats

For the ultimate in small-boat racing, nothing can equal the planing-type hull. Properly handled, it will lift itself out of the water, become partially air-borne, and take off at spectacular speeds. Planing sailboats generally have flat hulls—particularly aft of amidships—and must be as light as possible. They are, therefore, highly engineered, tend to be fragile and require sensitive, skillful handling.

SUNFISH

The largest racing class in the world is the Sunfish. It is a development of the original sailing surfboard—called a Sailfish— but is larger, at 14 feet over all, and has a small footwell. It is a basically simple design with a daggerboard and lateen sail. Strict class rules keep the oldest Sunfish competitive with new ones and limit expensive gadgets. Cost is under $800.

Each year there is a Sunfish World

The Sunfish, a development of the original sailing surfboard, is now the world's largest one-design racing class. (Courtesy Bermuda News Bureau)

Championship which attracts the top sailors from all over the world. One hundred identical new boats are provided for the series.

Besides exciting racing, the Sunfish provides well over 60,000 sailors with thrilling planing, off-the-beach sailing and just plain "hacking around" fun. It is rugged and easy to maintain.

LASER

Designed in 1970 by Bruce Kirby to be a "second generation" off-the-beach boat, the Laser demonstrated that it was right on target and enjoyed phenomenal growth as soon as it was introduced. It attracted top racing skippers from many different classes—some of whom race it as a "sec-

ond" boat. Over 5,000 Lasers were built and sold in the first two years, and the International Yacht Racing Union, in an unprecedented move for a new class developed independently, granted it International status in 1972, thereby paving the way for Olympic competition.

The design concept of the Laser called for a more modern racing machine than the then current off-the-beach boats. It has a modern, high aspect ratio Marconi sail; an aerodynamically shaped and raked daggerboard and rudder, and a rounded efficiently shaped planing hull. Yet, class rules are quite strict and prohibit the addition of expensive gadgets.

The Laser is 13 feet, 11 inches over all; is built of fiberglass; weighs 125 pounds and carries a single sail of 76 square feet. Cost is about $800 in 1974.

The Laser is one of the fastest growing classes. The class was granted International status just a year and a half after its introduction. (Photo by Sue Cummings)

The Fireball is popular among both advanced juniors and adults. (Courtesy Modern Boating)

FIREBALL

A high-performance sailboat that can be home-built of plywood, the Fireball was designed in 1962 by Englishman Peter Milne. The Fireball enjoys steady but unspectacular growth, numbering over 7,000 world wide. It is 16 feet, 2 inches over all; has a relatively narrow 4-foot, 9-inch beam; weighs 175 pounds and carries 124 square feet of sail plus a spinnaker.

Fireballs are very exciting to sail—ideal for a husband and wife. The crew may use a trapeze wire to hike out over the water for additional stability. It is an International Class eligible for Olympic selection. New fiberglass Fireballs cost about $2,000, and they are available in kit form either in fiberglass or wood in various

stages of assembly for less than $500. The Fireball is also the official junior boat in several areas.

470

Similar in performance to the Fireball but completely different in appearance and construction, the 470 is a modern, high-performance, planing sailboat designed by Frenchman André Cornu in 1964. It, too, was slow to catch on, but its numbers spread to well over 11,000 after ten years. Olympic status, conferred in 1972, further boosted the 470's popularity.

Construction was designed for fiberglass, and the design takes advantage of that material's ability to conform to compound curves, rolled tanks, and flared top-sides. Also, every conceivable "go-fast" gadget is incorporated into most 470s so that helmsman and crew have complete control of sails, spars, centerboard, and rudder.

The 470 is 15 feet, 6 inches over all, weighs 245 pounds, and sets 137 square feet of sail plus spinnaker. The crew hikes from a trapeze wire. Cost is about the same as a fiberglass Fireball at about $2,000 complete.

These are just a very few of the popular sailboat racing classes from which to choose; over 500 one-design classes are raced throughout the world. Perhaps the most important consideration when deciding what class boat to buy is to choose the one that is raced most actively at your club or in your local area. You must also consider your own personal needs and requirements as covered in Chapter 1. It would be silly to buy a three-man Soling because Solings are the strongest local fleet if you intend to sail single-handed. Pick the boat that suits you best from among those raced nearby.

The 470, a modern fiberglass two-man one-design, is one of the six Olympic classes. (*Courtesy Sailboats '73*)

Chapter 7

THE CRUISING SAILBOAT

In the last decade, sailing has increased at a greater rate than all other forms of boating. During that same period, the population of small cruising sailboats—boats with bunks and at least some minimal living accommodations—has exploded. In 1966 *One-Design & Offshore Yachtsman* magazine listed 40 cruising sailboats under 30 feet in their annual catalogue. In 1973 the same publisher listed over 200 classes of such boats that *were not listed in 1966*. No one knows for sure how many of these boats are sailing, but it is estimated that by 1970—or soon thereafter—there were more small cruising boats in the United States than any other kind of sailboat.

It will not be possible to describe the many different types, but an explanation of their design concept and function should show the reason for their wide and ever-increasing popularity.

A small cruising sailboat, which is rather arbitrarily and inadequately defined as one under 30 feet over-all length that has a self-draining cockpit and some sort of living accommodations, can be used in a variety of ways. Most are intended for short cruises—overnight, weekend, a week of "harbor hopping"—and some can make extended offshore passages. Because

of their small size, these cruisers can also be used conveniently as day sailers; they are easy to handle, can be gotten under way and secured quickly and have sufficient cockpit and deck space to accommodate a number of adults comfortably. The cabin provides a dry area to store clothing, a picnic lunch and a place to retreat in case of bad weather. The small cruising sailboat conveniently serves two purposes —cruising and day sailing.

Strangely, this dual purpose sailboat costs little more than a single-purpose day sailer. The reason for this is that the day sailer is often designed, equipped, and sold as a racing boat with correspondingly complicated and expensive equipment. Also, when both the modern day sailer and the cruising sailboat of the same size are examined, it becomes apparent that there is little difference in terms of structure or weight between the two. Therefore, it is logical that they should cost about the same. As an example, consider a typical keel day sailer. It is made of fiberglass; is 19 feet, 2 inches over all and has a small, open, shelter cuddy. Its price is $2,495 not including sails, life jackets, anchor, anchor line, dock lines, and miscellaneous necessary small items. A 21-foot, 8-inch cruising sailboat with four

TARTAN 27 *fiberglass cruising auxiliary. Length over all, 27 feet; waterline, 21 feet, 5 inches; beam, 8 feet, 7½ inches; displacement, 6,500 pounds. (Courtesy Douglass & McLeod)*

berths in an enclosed cabin, an icebox, lockers and place for a stove—built by the same company—costs $2,795. The same additional equipment will have to be added to this boat at, perhaps, slightly higher cost, but for only 15 percent greater cost, one obtains a sailboat with a great many more uses.

Even those interested in racing can do so with a small cruising sailboat. There are active fleets in which different designs compete on a handicap basis. Usually this means that each boat is measured to determine its potential speed. The measurements are converted to a "rating" by means of mathematical formulae, and the rating—usually expressed in feet to approximate waterline length—is converted to a handicap either through "time allowance tables" or performance curves that have been pre-computed. The time allowance handicap is expressed in units of time. To win, a boat must finish within the time allowed it by all boats with a higher handicap and finish ahead of all with a lower handicap by an amount of time greater than the allowance given them. This sounds terribly complicated, and it is, although the beginner need not worry about how ratings and handicaps are determined.

In spite of ever-increasing complication of the rating systems, they don't always work. So far, they have been unable to account for advantages gained by particular types of boats in particular types of races and weather patterns. It is sometimes true that the best-sailed and fastest boat *doesn't* win. Still, there are two more types of races open to owners of small cruising sailboats that overcome this problem and can be just as satisfying as racing a one-design day sailer.

One system that has recently become popular in Europe and appears to be spreading to other parts of the world is called "level racing."

Level racing is competition among boats with the same rating—therefore the same theoretical speed—without time allowance. Just like one-design racing, the first boat to finish is the winner. Each boat must be measured and must have a rating to determine what class it must sail in, but the rating is not converted to a time allowance. There are five classes recognized internationally for cruising sailboats rating 18, 21.7, 24.5, 27.5, and 32 to the International Offshore Rule. These ratings correspond very generally to a boat's waterline length in feet; the first three falling within our definition of "small cruising sailboat."

When there are enough series-built boats to form a one-design class of cruising sailboats, owners of these boats are able to race against each other without either time allowance or rating. In this case all the boats are either identical or so nearly alike that there should be no difference in speed. These boats can race just as the one-design day sailers do. Removing the variable of boat speed, the smartest and most agile crew wins. This is the theory, at least, although it does not account for luck, which is always a factor in any sailboat race.

In addition to the advantages of being able to day sail, cruise, or race in a small cruising sailboat, many of them can be trailered. Trailering will be discussed in detail in Chapter 24. In brief, trailering increases the range of any sailboat and can reduce the cost of maintenance by allowing the boat to be stored at home.

The cost of a small cruising sailboat will vary considerably. Quite naturally, the larger boats cost more, but there seems to be a break-off point beyond which the initial purchase price leaps from a few thousand dollars to over $10,000. As soon as a boat becomes large enough for adults to stand upright in the cabin, the cost soars. This is not a direct causal relationship so much as an over-all indication of size, or volume—which is a more significant measure of cost than over-all length. In addition, a larger boat will probably have more equipment installed: a stove, more berths, a toilet, basins, water tanks and even an inboard engine, all of which add considerably to the cost.

The intended use will also have an effect on cost. A boat that will be used almost exclusively for day sailing will not need a stove, toilet or water tanks—which will be required if one wants to go cruising, even for a weekend. A boat which is only intended for day sailing or cruising will not need expensive racing equipment. However, one of the less obvious advantages of a small cruising sailboat is that it can start out as a day sailer—at minimum cost—and be upgraded to cruiser and racer simply by adding equipment as the need arises and the budget allows.

Chapter 8

SPECIAL TYPES OF SAILBOAT

The Catamaran

Although the catamaran type of sailing craft has been in use for over a thousand years, it reached its present high state of development very recently. Twin hulls, long, narrow, and very light, are tied together by a platform or deck, which serves as a "cockpit." Cat- or sloop-rigged, the mainsail has full-length battens to achieve a nearly perfect airfoil under all conditions. Unlike early models which were rather indifferent performers beating against the wind, the newer catamarans

The new CATFISH, *with high-speed rudders. Designed by George Patterson and built by Alcort. (Courtesy Alcort, Inc.)*

Windsurfer is a true modern surfboard with a sail that is manipulated directly with the hands, arms, and body. Steering is accomplished by moving the feet and shifting body weight. (Courtesy Yacht Racing)

perform well to windward and in a strong breeze on a reach, with the wind nearly abeam, they take off at a fantastic speed, and the sensation is one of flying over the water rather than through it.

Most catamarans used for racing or day sailing run from 12 to 24 feet, and speeds of 20 knots or better when reaching are common. Built of fiberglass or plywood, they are available in kit form, and prices start around $800 and go up to about $3,000.

The Board Boat

The board boat type started life in 1947 with the design of the Sailfish. It was nothing more than a glorified surfboard with a sail, something for children to play around with at the beach. In a very short time some owners saw the sporting possibilities, and started racing. The Sunfish, which is described in a previous chapter, is a development of this original board boat, and today there are tens of thousands of Sailfish, Sunfish, and their copies and derivatives sailing throughout the world.

One interesting development of the board boat concept is the Windsurfer. This is literally a surfboard with a sail. The Windsurfer has no rudder or centerboard (a small fixed fin provides lateral resistance) and is steered with foot and body position, just like a surfboard. The mast is pivoted on a universal joint and is held up by the "helmsman" who hangs onto a wishbone boom.

Hulls of board boats are generally of plywood, fiberglass, or foam plastic. They are watertight, and they have wood or metal centerboard and rudder.

Sails are simple lateen or gunter, with aluminum spars. Some makes have a well, or "cockpit," which is just big enough for your feet. One attractive feature of the board boats is their portability—you can slide one into your station wagon or tie it on your cartop carrier.

The two basic requirements in sailing the board boats are physical agility and a bathing suit. In anything but the lightest winds they capsize easily and frequently. When this happens, you grab the high side, put your foot against the centerboard, crawl aboard as she comes upright, and carry on. No pumping or bailing or tangled gear and little lost time; just a quick dunking and you're sailing again in less than a minute.

Because of their light weight and low initial stability, it takes considerable agility to keep board boats on their feet and sailing efficiently. In the puffs they accelerate very quickly and plane easily if handled smartly. Since you are literally sailing "by the seat of your pants," the sensation of speed over and through the water is really something to experience.

Several types of board boats are available in kit form, with prices starting under $100. Complete boats cost $300 to $600.

The Sailing Dinghy

Dinghies come in an infinite variety of shapes, sizes, and materials, and most of them can be rowed, sailed, or powered by outboard. They are made of fiberglass, plastic, sheet plywood, molded plywood, aluminum, or lapstrake planks.

Perhaps the most popular type is the two-transom, or square-ended pram. For a given length, the pram has the greatest capacity, can carry the biggest load, and is the most stable.

Where a dinghy serves as a tender for a small cruiser, with its attendant stowage problem, size and weight limitations are

The Dyer Dhow is one of the most popular dual-purpose boats, serving as a sailing dinghy—often used in "frostbiting" races—and tender for larger yachts. (Photo by John Hopf, courtesy The Anchorage, Inc.)

of prime importance. Here the pram of around 7 feet in length is ideal. You can row the dog ashore for his daily constitutional or take the whole crew visiting via outboard, and the youngsters can step the mast and go for a sail when approaching boredom.

The sailing rig is the simple jib-headed cat, with the mast often in two sections, jointed, so that it can be stowed within the boat. Centerboard is the removable dagger type.

Prices for a completed dinghy, with sail, run from around $400 to $500 or more. Kits are available in some makes at a considerable saving in cost.

Chapter 9

LEARNING TO SAIL

There are two ways to acquire knowledge of a skill—by study and by doing. Reading and memorizing a book is not going to make you a sailor. You have to get out in a boat and sail, and gather firsthand experience.

Ask an experienced sailor to go out with you a few times and show you how. He can correct your mistakes, explain what is happening and why, and help to eliminate the worry and indecision you would experience if you were alone. Book study complements personal instruction. It helps you to learn the theory and basic elements of sailing, and their practical application. It enables you to recognize facts and situations when they occur, and the right way to meet them. The information you find in books represents many years of experience, and careful, intensive study will immeasurably shorten the process of becoming a sailor.

Nomenclature

In learning to sail you'll not only need a boat, but a vocabulary to go with it. All parts of a boat, the areas about them, and all sailing attitudes have names known and used by sailors everywhere.

You'll need to know them in order to understand what we are talking about. Nautical terminology is not a fetish, it is necessary for the efficient and safe operation of any boat, large or small. Spoken orders must be concisely given and clearly understood; "that rope over there" is not very specific.

In the British Navy they have a saying, "The bottom of this box is marked TOP, in order to avoid confusion." So, to avoid confusion, study the following diagrams and learn the proper names.

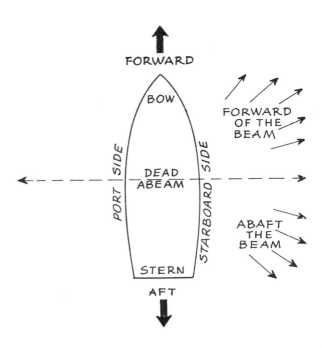

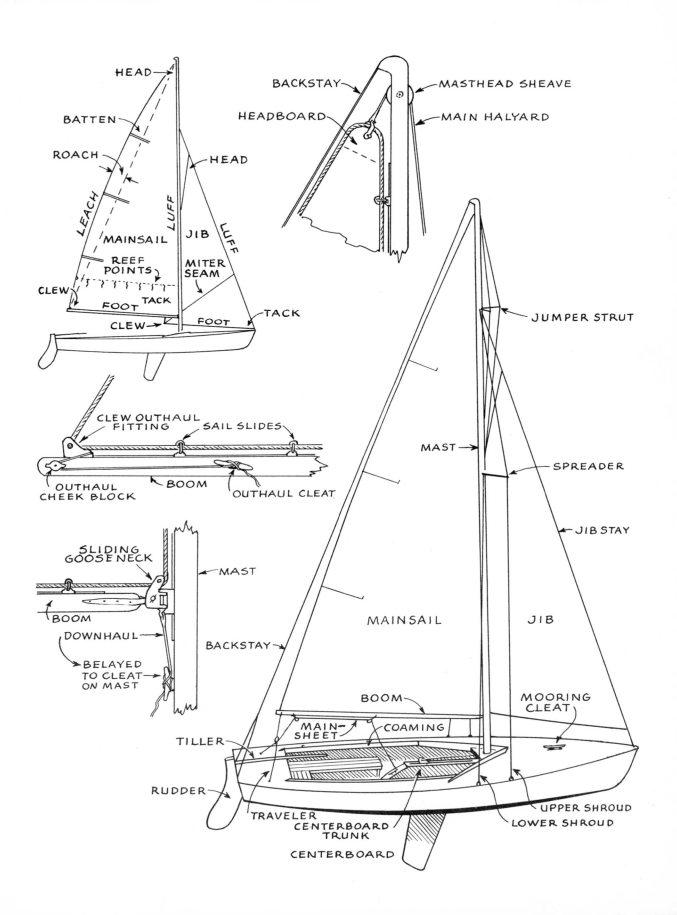

In this, as in most books on sailing, wind direction in the illustrations is indicated by arrows. (The arrows in the accompanying "forward and aft" diagram represent directions, not winds, however.) But when you are out sailing, you'll look in vain for a flock of arrows flying through the sky, and you'll have to depend on other means. The hardest thing for a beginner to learn, and the one thing he seems oblivious to, is the direction of the wind *in relation to the boat's heading.*

Since the course you steer and the trim of your sails depends entirely on wind direction, the sooner you learn to judge it correctly, the better. You'll never be a *good* sailor until you do.

Apparent Wind

There are two "kinds" of wind—*true* and *apparent.* The true wind is the wind that blows across the water in the immediate vicinity of your boat. The apparent wind is the deflected wind that results from your boat moving against (or across) the true wind. The apparent wind will be stronger, and come more from ahead, than the true wind.

It can be expressed by laying out a *parallelogram of forces,* as in the diagram. Let's assume the true wind force is 8 knots, and your boat is sailing on the wind at 3 knots. The line AB represents the boat's course and speed, and AC indicates the direction and force of the true wind. If the line BD is projected parallel to AC, the resultant vector, AD, is the direction of the *apparent wind,* and its force is about 9½ knots.

At all times when sailing, the sails must be trimmed in relation to the *apparent* wind, not the true wind. Therefore it is essential to know its exact direction every minute, and the only way you can find out is by looking at the *masthead fly.*

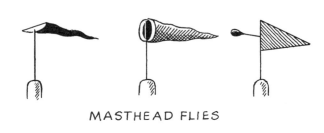

MASTHEAD FLIES

There are numerous masthead flies available—a cloth triangular pennant, a cone-shaped wind sock, or a metal or plastic fly, weighted on the forward edge so it is balanced. The last-named type is the best, since it will not flutter like a flag.

Telltales—bits of ribbon or yarns on the shrouds—also show the direction of the apparent wind, and are useful when you are beating to windward. But off the

TRUE WIND

APPARENT WIND

A   BOAT'S COURSE   B

C   D

wind, particularly in running, the mast-head fly is more accurate.

Preparation

Before bending sail, be sure your boat is properly equipped. Never go out unless the following are aboard: an approved life jacket for each person, an anchor and suitable length of cable, an oar or paddle, and a bilge pump or bailer. And remember that a good sailor carries a stout knife on his person at all times. The sailor's sheath knife is best, worn on your belt just abaft your right hip; it is ready at hand in an instant, and you don't have to open it.

Upon boarding your boat, let the centerboard down and attach your rudder and tiller. If your boat has a wire mainsheet traveler, make sure the tiller is *under* the traveler. See that both the main and jib sheets are not cleated, or tangled, but free to run out at will.

Never bend or hoist sails unless the boat is lying head-to-the-wind. If moored at a dock with bow and stern lines, cast off the stern line and the boat will swing into the wind, like a weathervane. If the wind is blowing the boat *against* the dock, take her around to the other side, or paddle her over to some convenient place where she can lie head-to-wind.

You are now ready to bend on the sails —which, of course, are in a sail bag. The mainsail goes on first, the jib last. There's a right and a wrong way for everything —always remember that the headboard is the last to go in the bag when stowing, so that it's the first part to come out. Now, starting at the headboard, feed the slides on the track one by one, and be sure you don't skip any. When all are on, the whole business would slide down and off the track unless held in some fashion. Most

boats have a latch or turn button at the bottom of the track for this purpose; if yours has none, tie a line temporarily around the mast just above the end of the track. Shackle on the halyard, first looking aloft to be sure the halyard runs free and is not fouled around the rigging or spreaders.

With the luff of the sail on the track, the next step is to shackle the tack to the gooseneck fitting. Now, starting at the tack, overhaul the foot of the sail, by sliding it through your hands until you reach the clew, just to be sure the sail is not twisted. Put the slides on the boom track, making sure you aren't missing any, and haul the clew out to the end of the boom and attach the clew outhaul fitting. Now pull the clew outhaul *hand tight*. This means there should be no slack in the bolt rope along the foot of the sail, but you don't need a 150-pound pull, either. As a check, if vertical wrinkles appear, running upward from each sail slide, when the sail is hoisted, the outhaul is too slack. If so, take up just enough strain to eliminate them. Tie a stop, or piece of line around the sail and boom temporarily to keep the sail from spilling into the boat.

Now the battens should be put in. Since the leach of the sail has a "roach," meaning it is cut in a convex curve, battens are needed to extend the leach, otherwise it would curl inward. The battens are not all the same length, and therefore it is a good idea to mark them, TOP, MIDDLE, and BOTTOM. Thus you are always sure which batten goes in each pocket.

Bend the jib on next. Shackle on the tack first, then hook on each jib-snap in turn, and finally shackle the halyard onto the headboard, again making sure the halyard is not fouled. See that the jib sheets are clear, and not twisted, and tie them to the clew.

You are now ready to hoist the mainsail. Check again to see that the boat is lying head-to-wind, and the mainsheet is clear so that the boom is free to swing back and forth unhindered. Hoist the sail up smartly, and take a half-turn on the cleat. Now look up the luff of the sail, and set up on the halyard until wrinkles appear, running diagonally upward a foot or so from each sail slide. Rope stretches under strain, and when the sail is filled with wind these wrinkles will disappear. Make the halyard fast with several crossing turns on the cleat, and secure with a half-hitch. Now unship the boom crotch and stow it away under the deck.

Next hoist the jib in like manner and belay the halyard. Again, be sure there is plenty of slack in the jib sheets, so that the jib is able to swing back and forth freely.

You are now ready to shove off and get under way. Look around you to be sure no boats are approaching, and that the area into which you will sail is free of traffic.

If there are no other boats docked alongside of you, take off your dock line and shove the bow off, sideways, away from the wind. Step quickly to the tiller, pull your main and jib sheets in a bit, and as the wind fills the sails the boat will pick up speed, and you are on your way.

But if boats are docked on either side of you, the procedure is different. The best thing to do is to get someone on the dock to cast off your dock line and shove the boat directly backward, while you remain at the tiller. As soon as you are clear of the other boats, put your tiller hard over to one side, so the rudder will swing the stern around. When the boat is crosswise to the wind, trim in the main and jib sheets, and the boat will start moving ahead.

The diagram shows these two methods of getting away from a dock.

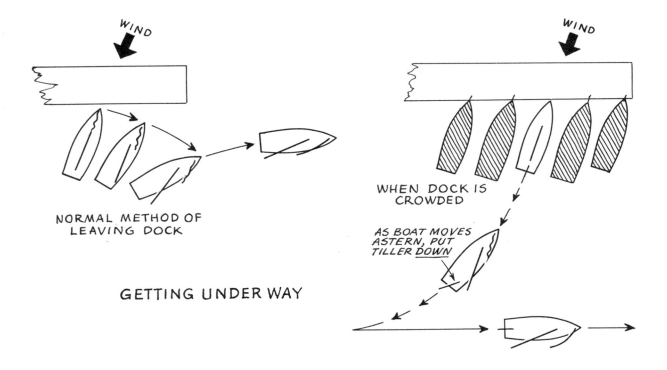

NORMAL METHOD OF
LEAVING DOCK

GETTING UNDER WAY

WHEN DOCK IS
CROWDED

AS BOAT MOVES
ASTERN, PUT
TILLER *DOWN*

Sailing to Windward

Suppose we leave the boat and skipper in a state of suspended animation while we consider what is going to happen and why. Before actually sailing off, it is necessary to understand the basic theory of sailing—how the boat is steered, the effect of the wind on the sails, and how the sails should be trimmed.

First consider the rudder and tiller. Beginners are often confused by the fact that

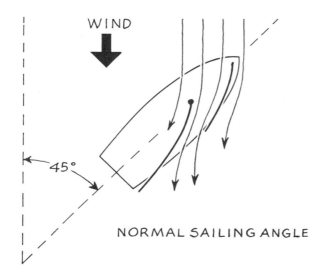

NORMAL SAILING ANGLE

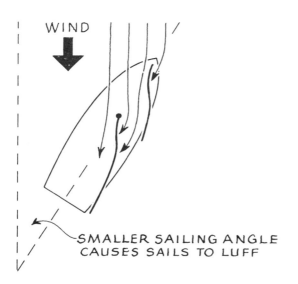

SMALLER SAILING ANGLE
CAUSES SAILS TO LUFF

a boat is not steered like an automobile. Pushing the tiller to one side makes the boat turn toward the other side. "Put the tiller (or helm) down," means to push it *with* the wind; the rudder will turn the boat *into the wind*. To turn the boat away from, or off the wind, you put the tiller *up,* or toward the wind.

The boat cannot be steered or turned unless it is moving. Speed through the water means *control*. There is nothing more ludicrous than the sight of a beginner in a motionless boat with sails shaking in the wind, pumping the tiller back and forth, while he wonders why the boat doesn't turn in either direction.

When the wind fills the sail, it takes a gentle curve, called an airfoil shape, similar to an airplane wing section. The maximum "belly," or depth of the curve is about a third of the way back from the luff of the sail.

A boat cannot sail directly against the wind. It cannot sail much closer than an angle of 45 degrees. Any attempt to sail closer will cause the sail to *luff,* which means the wind strikes the lee side of the sail just ahead of the "belly," causes the sail to flutter, and destroys the airfoil shape. (In racing, to "luff up" means to quickly head up closer to the wind, which, of course, kills the boat's speed.)

So, as the diagram shows, when you want to sail to a point directly upwind, you get there by *tacking,* making a series of short "hitches" or tacks, first to one side of the wind, then coming about and sailing awhile to the other side. Note that the boat sails 45 degrees to the wind, but the course is changed 90 degrees each time the boat tacks, or comes about.

When the boat's course is to the *right* of the wind direction, it is on the *port tack,* since the wind hits the sails on the port side, while the boom and sail are on the

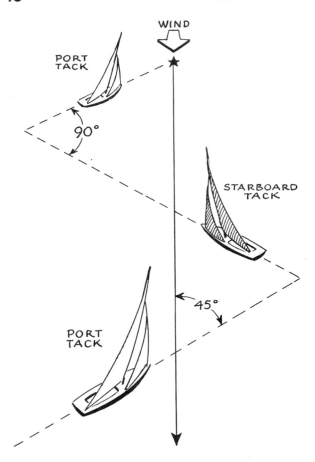

WIND

PORT
TACK

90°

STARBOARD
TACK

45°

PORT
TACK

lee, or starboard side. When you come
about, bringing the wind on the other side
of the sail, you are on the *starboard tack,*
and the new course is 90 degrees from
the old.

How close do you trim the sails when
sailing close-hauled, or close to the wind?
This will vary with the force of the wind
and the cut or shape of the sails. The
harder it blows, the flatter the sail should
be, and the closer you can trim it. In light
airs, the sail should have greater draft, or
belly, and it shouldn't be trimmed in as
close. Generally speaking, when sailing as
close to the wind as possible, the mainsail
will be trimmed to bring the boom just
over the corner of the stern, or transom.

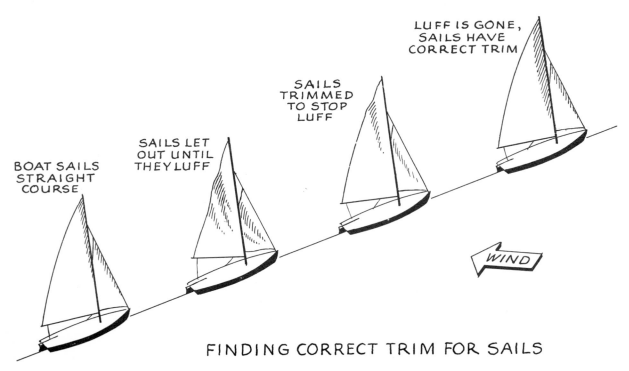

BOAT SAILS
STRAIGHT
COURSE

SAILS LET
OUT UNTIL
THEY LUFF

SAILS
TRIMMED
TO STOP
LUFF

LUFF IS GONE,
SAILS HAVE
CORRECT TRIM

WIND

FINDING CORRECT TRIM FOR SAILS

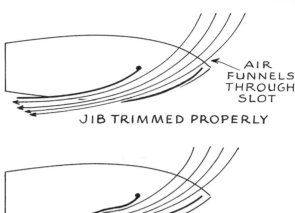

JIB TRIMMED PROPERLY

AIR FUNNELS THROUGH SLOT

AIRFLOW DEFLECTED INTO MAINSAIL CAUSES <u>LUFF</u>

JIB TRIMMED IN TOO FAR

Getting Under Way

Now let us go back to where we were, shoving off from the dock and getting under way. Since you are not racing, and can sail where you will, steer the boat on a course a little off the wind, or somewhat more than 45 degrees, with the sail eased off a bit. The reason for not trimming the sails in flat, or steering so close to the wind, is to pick up speed rapidly, so that the boat will respond more positively to the action of the tiller.

To *correct* the trim of the sails for your particular heading, steer a straight course and let the mainsail out slowly, until a slight luff appears. Then trim the sail in until the luff just disappears, and no farther. Make the sheet fast with a few turns on the cleat, and consider the jib. The jib has two sheets—a windward one and one to leeward. The windward sheet must be slack at all times—free to run at will. Ease the leeward sheet out slowly until a slight luff or flutter starts up near the

head, then trim in until it just stops. Your mainsail and jib are now trimmed to work most effectively on the course you are steering.

As the diagrams show, there is an "air slot" between the jib and the mainsail. The funneling of air through this narrow slot gives drive and power to your sails. In sailing to windward, it is imperative that this slot be preserved. If you trim the jib in too far, it will "backwind" the mainsail—the slot becomes restricted and the wind will be deflected against the "belly" of the sail, causing it to luff.

With the sails drawing beautifully and the boat slipping along smoothly, you might think you can relax and enjoy the scenery. Not so! The wind constantly varies in direction and strength, and the sails must be adjusted to meet the changes. Keep an eye on the upper part of your mainsail. If it starts to luff while you are steering a straight course, you are being "headed"—the wind has shifted more ahead, so you must bear off a bit to stop the luff.

If the wind is more abeam, there will be no telltale luff, but you'll notice the boat suddenly heels more, and there's more pull on the tiller. If so, luff up a bit to take advantage of it by sailing closer to the wind, or "pointing higher."

Suddenly a strong puff, or "flaw," hits you, and the boat heels alarmingly with greatly increased pressure on the tiller. This is a "knockdown," and you respond instantly by slacking off the main sheet, at the same time luffing up. The boat will come back on her feet, and when the flaw has passed on you pay off onto your original course, and trim in the mainsail to where it was before.

This points up one of the cardinal principles of small-boat sailing. *Never* belay the main sheet by taking a half-hitch on the cleat. Take a single turn around the cleat to relieve the strain, and hold the sheet in your hand at all times. Thus you can slack off the sheet *instantly* if a puff strikes. And always be alert to be sure the remainder of the sheet lies free and clear on the cockpit floor, ready to run out in an instant. Don't let your feet, or anything else, get fouled up in it.

It is now time to go about onto the other tack, and we'll assume you have a crew tending the jib sheet. The skipper warns his crew of the maneuver with the hail "Ready about!" and takes a quick look to windward to see that the area is clear and no boats nearby. At the command "Hard alee!" he puts the helm down, *gradually*. The crew has the jib sheet in his hand watching the luff of the jib, and as the boom starts to swing over, both men move smoothly to the other side of the boat. The crew keeps the jib trimmed in until he sees it start to luff, then lets the sheet fly free. He waits until the boat falls off on her new tack, then trims the jib in with the *other* jib sheet.

The secret in coming about is to keep the boat moving and to *sail* the boat around by proper use of the rudder. Don't suddenly shove the tiller hard over—this causes the rudder to act as a brake and kills the speed of the boat. In light airs it can stop the boat dead in her tracks.

The correct way is to put the tiller down gradually and smoothly, not as far as it can go, but somewhere in between, say 45 degrees from the centerline of the boat. The boat's course should describe a slow arc, smoothly and evenly with no loss of forward speed.

The beginner often "stalls" the boat when trying to come about. He starts the maneuver with not enough speed to carry through, and when the boat comes head

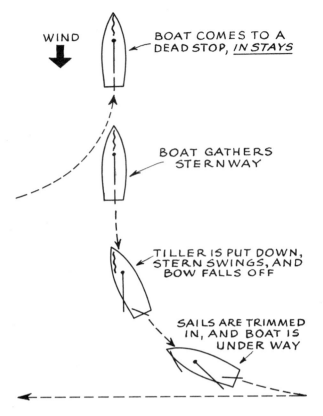

WIND

BOAT COMES TO A DEAD STOP, *IN STAYS*

BOAT GATHERS STERNWAY

TILLER IS PUT DOWN, STERN SWINGS, AND BOW FALLS OFF

SAILS ARE TRIMMED IN, AND BOAT IS UNDER WAY

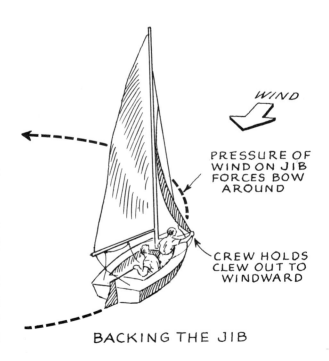

WIND

PRESSURE OF WIND ON JIB FORCES BOW AROUND

CREW HOLDS CLEW OUT TO WINDWARD

BACKING THE JIB

to the wind she stops dead, with the sails fluttering, and the rudder is then useless. This is called "getting in stays," or "in irons." The only remedy is to back the jib immediately by taking hold of the clew and holding it out against the wind. This should swing the bow over on the other tack.

If you are not quick enough backing the jib, the boat may start to gather sternway, or move directly backward. In this case, put the tiller over toward the side you wish to sail away on, and the rudder will swing the stern around. Then bring the tiller up, trim sheets, and you are on your way again.

Reaching

There are three sailing "attitudes," beating, reaching, and running. As we have seen, when a boat is sailing as close to the wind as possible, she is "on the wind," or *beating*—with the sails trimmed in close (close-hauled) and the wind over the bow. When the wind is coming from directly astern, the boat is *running,* or sailing free. On all points between beating and running, she is *reaching*. With the wind forward of the beam, the boat is on a *close reach,* and if it is abaft the beam, she is on a *broad reach.*

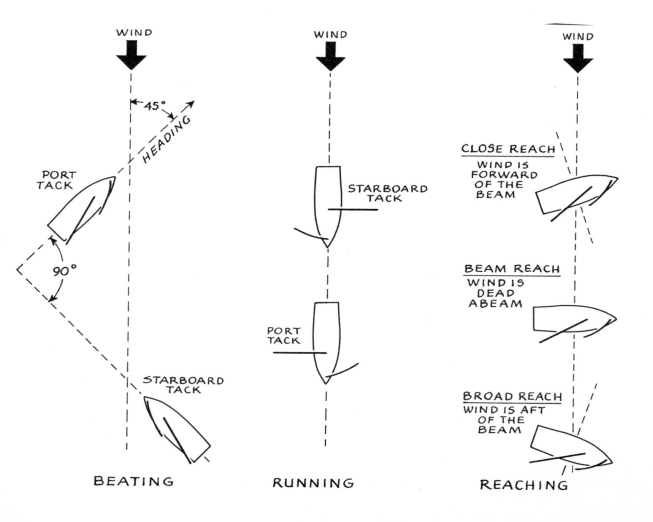

BEATING   RUNNING   REACHING

A boat travels fastest when reaching, and it is the easiest and most enjoyable part of sailing. The sails are trimmed for reaching by the same method as in beating—the sheets are eased out until a slight luff appears, then trimmed in until the luff barely disappears. It cannot be emphasized too strongly that a good sailor sails his boat at top speed, and with maximum efficiency at all times, whether he is racing or not. Therefore, whether you are beating, reaching, or running, the sails should be trimmed at all times as close to the wind as possible, without luffing!

Tacking from a reach is almost impossible—for if you were to put the helm down you would get in stays long before the boat came head-to-the-wind. To change tacks on a reach you must first round up slowly, trimming the sails in as you do so, until you are close-hauled. Then go about, as previously described.

Jibing

Jibing is changing tacks while sailing downwind—on a broad reach or running. More small-boat sailors get into trouble trying to jibe than at any other time. Dismastings, capsizings, and torn sails are invariably the result of improper jibing techniques. The best way to learn to jibe smoothly and safely is to pick a day when the wind is light, and *practice,* again and again until you are proficient.

Let us assume you are on the starboard tack, on a broad reach. Before starting the maneuver, look to see that the mainsheet is clear and ready to run, and note the exact wind direction in relation to the boat's heading. Now put your helm up slowly, and as the boat comes directly before the wind, haul in the mainsheet smartly. With the boom dead amidships, and the sail flat,

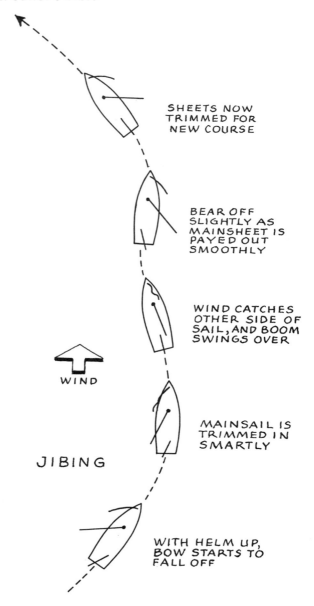

SHEETS NOW TRIMMED FOR NEW COURSE

BEAR OFF SLIGHTLY AS MAINSHEET IS PAYED OUT SMOOTHLY

WIND CATCHES OTHER SIDE OF SAIL, AND BOOM SWINGS OVER

WIND

MAINSAIL IS TRIMMED IN SMARTLY

JIBING

WITH HELM UP, BOW STARTS TO FALL OFF

continue turning. When the wind catches the other side of the mainsail, pay out the sheet slowly as the boom swings out to starboard.

Now here is the most important part. As the mainsail swings out on the new tack, the boat has a tendency to swing quickly around with it and round up sharply into the wind. You must prevent this by putting the helm *up,* until she comes back on the desired course. If the boat is allowed to swing around unchecked, she will *broach,* or come around with such momentum that she lies over on her side with the sails dragging in the water, and may capsize.

With some small racing boats it is preferable to let the boom come over on the new tack without hauling in all of the sheet. Boats such as the Laser, Sunfish, and particularly the Olympic Finn, which have no standing rigging to catch battens, must be jibed this way in heavy weather to prevent a capsize. The vang must be tight to jibe with the boom sweeping rapidly across the deck, and be sure you remember to duck!

Running

Running is often referred to as "easy sailing," which it is not. The crew can take it easy and relax, but *not* the helmsman. The boat travels with or in the same direction as the wind. Theoretically the boat travels at the same speed as the wind, minus the resistance of the hull pushing through the water. There is little sail-handling required, but the waves coming up from astern tend to swing the stern around first one way then the other, and the boat is said to "yaw." This means the helmsman must be alert every minute, meeting and even anticipating the swing of the boat with the rudder, to hold the boat on a straight course down wind.

The mainsail is carried as far out as possible, without riding or rubbing against the lee shroud, which means an angle of something less than 90 degrees to the wind. The jib, which is blanketed by the mainsail, would do no work if left to its own devices. So we put it to work by means of a *whisker pole.* One end of the pole hooks into a fitting on the mast, and the other

end hooks into the clew of the jib; thus the jib is held out and is drawing on the side opposite to the mainsail. This is called "winging out" the jib. Old-time sailors in the days of the coasting schooners referred to it as "wung out."

There is one very real danger in running before the wind—the accidental jibe. It is caused by sailing *below* the true course, or axis of the wind, and is called "sailing by the lee." The wind may get behind the leach of the mainsail and cause a sudden, violent jibe, "all standing," and something may carry away in the process. Capsizing is not unlikely. The way to avoid such an occurrence is fairly obvious —*never* sail by the lee. Be everlastingly vigilant—watch your wind pennant and the telltales on your shrouds for wind shifts. The wind direction is never constant, it is continually veering back and forth. Sometimes the shifts are very slight, and again they may run as high as 15 or 20 degrees. Don't ignore them, meet the

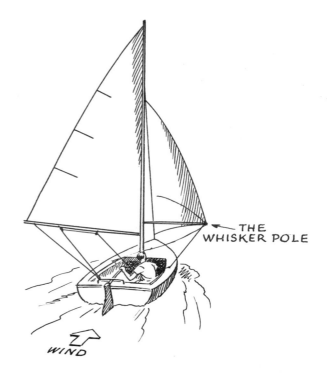

THE WHISKER POLE

WIND

shifts with the helm. In running, when the wind shifts from dead astern to over the lee quarter, or the same side the mainsail is carried on, put the helm down instantly, to bring the boat's course directly before the "new" wind.

There is another aspect of the accidental jibe which is not only startling, but downright dangerous to the boat and gear. That is the "goosewing" jibe, in which the boom and lower part of the mainsail jibe over violently, while the upper part of the sail does not. The harder the wind the more liable it is to happen. The wind gets behind the lower part of the sail, near the boom end, and with the sheet all out and untended, the boom flies up in the air and over in a high arc. The head of the sail stays where it is, so half of the sail is on one side and half on the other. This can be prevented by keeping the vang tight (see page 72).

If this does happen to you, what to do? You can't head up or luff, for the upper part of the sail only presses harder on the spreaders, and the force exerted tends to keep the boat from heading up. The only way to get out of the mess is to *jibe back again,* then trim in the sheet and jibe properly. More often than not you'll not be so lucky. Broken boom, spreaders, and/or mast plus a torn sail are normal damages resulting from the goosewing jibe.

As stated earlier, running before the wind is "easy sailing," but *only in light to moderate winds.* As the wind increases in strength, so do the dangers. Therefore it is good seamanship to steer a little high of the course—in other words, more on a broad reach than dead before the wind. Thus there is less chance of an accidental jibe.

Heavy-Weather Sailing

Sailing in strong winds calls for different techniques in boat handling than you normally use in light weather. Good seamanship demands that you *favor* your boat—protect her (and yourself) from undue stress and strain as much as possible,

WIND

SAILING *BY THE LEE*
CAN RESULT IN A *GOOSEWING JIBE*

and get where you are going in maximum safety. There is an old saying that covers it: "The good seaman weathers the storm he cannot avoid, and avoids the storm he cannot weather."

JIB TRIMMED IN FLAT, MAINSAIL SLACKED OFF AND LUFFING

BEATING IN HEAVY WEATHER

First we'll consider beating to windward in strong winds. *Don't* sail as close-hauled as you can—if you luff when a puff hits you the boat will stop moving, because of the force of the waves, and with no forward speed you have no control. Thus the next puff can knock you flat! Remember, speed means control. Sail a little *off* the wind and keep the boat moving. Slack off the mainsheet to spill the wind, rather than luffing in the puffs. An old trick is to keep the jib trimmed in flat and ease the mainsheet out. Thus the jib backwinds the mainsail and spills some of the wind, while at the same time it keeps her moving ahead. "Play" the mainsheet constantly, slacking it off in the puffs, and trimming in in the lulls. If your boat is equipped

with an easily controlled traveler, keep the mainsheet tight and ease the traveler in the puffs.

The high wind is only half your trouble —you'll also be fighting heavy seas. With the bow pounding into the big ones, the wind is shaken out of the sails and forward speed is killed. About every fifth or seventh wave will be a big one. Don't let the boat slam into it—bear off to "give"

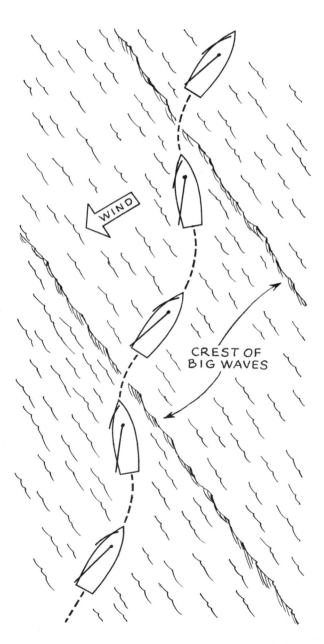

WIND

CREST OF BIG WAVES

with it, and come back on course as it passes under you. As the diagram shows, you "snake" your way to windward.

Another important element is the disposition of live ballast—which means you and your crew. The fore and aft trim of the boat affects the ability to drive to windward at the best possible speed. If you and your crew huddle together near the stern to avoid the spray, the bow rises and is forced away from the desired course, and forward speed is reduced. At the same time, the stern squats and creates a drag. Insist that your crew remain forward, and see that both of you hike out on the weather rail to counteract the heeling tendency.

Reaching in heavy weather is easier and more comfortable than beating, but it doesn't mean you can relax. It calls for real concentration on the helm, the trim of the sails, the wind and the seas. Your crew can move aft a bit to handle the mainsheet for you and let you concentrate on steering. The jib sheet can be cleated down, since pressure on the jib in the gusts will help to fight the boat's tendency to broach. The mainsheet must be held in the hands at all times, and "played" constantly. Ease it out until the mainsail has a slight luff at all times.

When a strong puff hits, slack off the sheet and bear off a bit with the helm. Thus you parry the broaching tendency and keep the boat footing. When you see a king-size wave about to hit, bear off with it, to lessen the blow, at the same time easing out the mainsheet.

When running to leeward in heavy winds, remember the advice previously given about the accidental jibe—*don't* sail directly down the axis of the wind, but steer high of the course to bring the wind over the weather quarter. You and your crew should sit all the way aft, to keep the bow high and the stern low. This makes the boat easier to steer, and keeps the bow from "rooting," or nosing under. In light to moderate winds the centerboard may be raised all the way up, but in heavy weather it should be carried about a third of the way down.

Reefing

As the wind increases there comes a time when a boat can no longer carry full sail, and it is necessary to reduce the sail area by reefing. Beginners seldom recognize that time when it comes. They carry on with too much sail until the boat is overpowered, and capsizing is often the outcome.

Notice the wind and water before you go out. If the water is covered with whitecaps, and any sailboats in sight are heeled way over, reefing is advisable. If in doubt, ask an experienced sailor.

If reefing is in order, be sure you understand how to do it the *right* way—improper reefing generally results in a torn or ruined sail. Follow these steps in their sequence, and study the diagrams. If you can get an experienced sailor to help you, so much the better.

1. Lower the sail all the way.

2. Start by tying the luff cringle so that it is directly alongside the tack cringle. This means taking a couple of turns with a stout lanyard through the luff cringle and around the boom at the gooseneck, then around the mast, securing it with a slipped reef knot. This lashing is called the *tack earing*.

3. Next tie a lanyard to the leach cringle, to serve as an outhaul. Reeve it through the hole in the boom end, haul the sail out snugly, and make fast to the clew outhaul cleat. Don't haul the sail out

too hard. It should be hand taut—with no more tension than the foot of the sail has.

4. Now pass a line through the leach cringle and around the boom, take a second turn and tie a reef knot. This is called the *reef earing.*

5. Pull out the loose part of the sail that lies between the reef points and the boom, called the *bunt,* and furl it snugly.

6. Starting at the luff, tie each set of reef points in turn. Pass the reef point that is on the far side of the sail *between* the sail and the boom, and tie the ends in a slipped reef knot. Make sure that each set of points is tied equally tight.

7. Now hoist the sail, secure the halyard, and notice how the sail sets. Small wrinkles reveal where the strain comes, and they should look identical at each set of reef points. If one set shows no wrinkles, it means the points have not been tied tight enough.

A sail can be ruined by improper reefing. Most of the strain should be borne by the tack and clew earings, rather than by the reef points. Therefore, be *sure* the clew and tack are held tightly down to the boom. If all the strain comes at the reef points, the cloth is unduly stretched.

Docking

Sailing a boat in to a dock, and stopping her exactly where you plan to land without ramming the dock or other boats already docked, can be a fine piece of boat handling, or a sickening spectacle. Sailboats don't have brakes like an auto, or reverse gears like a powerboat. Your motive power is the wind, and with proper sail-tending, you can turn it on or off at will. But bringing your boat to a dead stop at the exact spot and precise moment you desire is an art that you cannot expect to acquire overnight. It comes only with long experience and not until you have completely mastered your boat.

After days and weeks of sailing, hour after hour, under all conditions of wind and sea, your boat becomes a part of you. You know all her peculiarities—how she responds in every situation, when she needs babying, and when she needs a firm hand. You know what she can do and what her limitations are. You bend her to your will *not* by brute force, but by knowing how to make her do her best, without strain or effort. A good sailor has a sympathetic heart, and a sensitive hand.

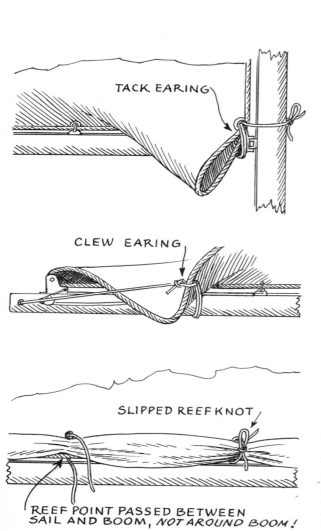

TACK EARING

CLEW EARING

SLIPPED REEF KNOT

REEF POINT PASSED BETWEEN SAIL AND BOOM, *NOT AROUND BOOM!*

As a prelude to learning how to dock your boat, you must learn how far she will "fetch." When you round up smartly head-to-wind, speed and momentum carry the boat forward, to windward, until she loses way and comes to a stop. She "coasts," in other words, and how far she will fetch depends on the weight of the boat, and the force of the wind. A heavy cruising-type boat will coast a considerable distance, but a Laser, for example, will practically come to a stop and not coast at all if a good breeze is blowing.

So let us suppose you have a light displacement boat, a small day sailer under 20 feet, and are about to bring her into the dock. The wind is light, 10 to 15 knots, and you are approaching on a reach. You note that while there are other boats at the dock, there is a clear space awaiting you, with plenty of room. Your crew is forward, jib sheet in hand, and a dock line is neatly coiled on the deck before him.

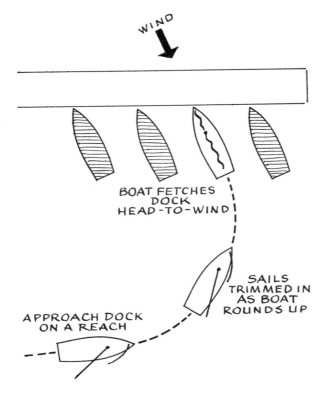

WIND

BOAT FETCHES
DOCK
HEAD-TO-WIND

SAILS
TRIMMED IN
AS BOAT
ROUNDS UP

APPROACH DOCK
ON A REACH

You round up into the wind, trimming in the mainsail as you do, in order to maintain headway, and as she comes dead-to-wind, both sheets are let fly, the sails fluttering like a weathervane, and if you have timed it right, your crew gets a line on the dock just as the boat comes to a stop.

This sounds easy, and as you study the diagram, it looks easy. Unfortunately, you are threatened by a number of ifs, buts, and howevers.

If you round up too soon, you won't fetch the dock, and the boat will be in irons. If this happens, your crew backs the jib for a moment, and the boat will fill away on a tack for another try. But, if you are *close* to the dock, this means trouble, since you could crash into the boat beside you.

If you round up too sharply, with too much speed, you can ram the dock. This is less dangerous, since your crew may be able to fend off, and you can damage only your own boat, not someone else's.

However, if you *did* time it right, there is still a danger to which you and your crew should be alert. *Don't for an instant* interfere with the free-swinging of the jib or mainsail. They must swing like a weathervane, for if the wind catches the sail on either side, the boat will gather speed and destroy your timing. If the jib catches the wind for a moment, it will swing the bow away, and your crew may just miss getting a line on the dock.

The best advice for the beginner is to practice. Try spotting your boat, over and over. Pick a day when the wind is moderate, and if possible, when the dock is free of other boats. Or practice fetching some other spot—a mooring buoy, a floating object, or even a stake in the water. Remember that you must always land *head-to-wind,* with no forward speed at moment of contact.

The Care of Your Boat

A good sailor keeps his boat neat, ship-shape, and orderly at all times, not only to protect his investment, but to insure safe and efficient performance.

Every rope end has a neat whipping, and all sheets and halyards are coiled down when not in use. Spare lines are coiled and stowed under deck, where they are readily available, and all loose gear is chocked off out of the way.

Keep your boat dry. Don't allow water to lie in the bilge—pump the boat out and sponge her dry after every sail. Rain water, if allowed to collect, is the main cause of rot. An inexpensive cockpit cover, or a tent-fly over the boom, keeps out sun, rain, and dirt, and reduces the labor of maintenance. Down close to the keel, every rib or floor timber has a small hole, close to the planking. These are called *limber holes,* and they were put there to allow water to drain down to the lowest part of the bilge, so that it can all be pumped out.

Invariably they become clogged with dirt and foreign matter, allowing pockets of water to accumulate. Keep a short piece of copper wire aboard, and clean out these limber holes each time you pump.

If fresh water is available where you keep your boat, hose her down or sponge off the accumulated salt spray each time you come in from a day's sail. This is especially important if the boat has much brightwork, since varnished surfaces are not as weather-resistant as painted or gel-coat surfaces.

If your boat is kept at a dock or float, see that fenders are rigged to prevent chafe. Rigging your mooring lines as shown in the diagrams will prevent serious damage in a bad storm. The boat is free to move around without hurting herself. And don't skimp on rope! Second-hand clothesline is not suitable for mooring—or for anything else aboard a boat. Your dock lines should be not less than ⅝ inch diameter if the boat is 20 feet or less. A 25-foot boat needs ¾ inch. Nylon or polypropylene is recommended, since both have high elasticity and strength.

Two views of boats moored to a dock. (Top photo by Hervey Garrett Smith, bottom photo courtesy Alcort, Inc.)

Chapter 10

MOORING AT A DOCK OR SLIP

When you are lying at a dock or in a slip, the safety of your boat depends on the proper disposition of the dock lines. The wash from a passing motorboat will cause your boat to surge violently, first one way and then the other. If she's lying comfortably in a southerly wind, she may bang and chafe badly when the wind shifts into the north.

moored at high water with not enough slack in the dock lines. When the tide drops, either the boat is "hung up" or the cleats are torn loose from the deck.

The *spring lines* keep the boat from surging back and forth. The more nearly they are parallel to the dock, the better.

Note the placement of fenders. A small boat can get along with one, but two are better.

The next diagram shows how to moor when the dock is very crowded, or on the windward side in a fresh breeze. In approaching the dock, round up, head-to-

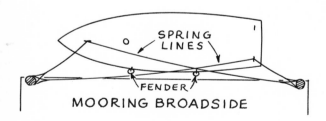

MOORING BROADSIDE

The first diagram shows a boat moored broadside to a dock. The *bow* and *stern lines* are secured to the nearest cleat or bollard on the dock, and they keep the boat in the broadside position. They should *never* be set up tight. At the time you make the lines fast, note the state of the tide, and allow enough slack for the rise and fall. All too often this is ignored, and a boat is

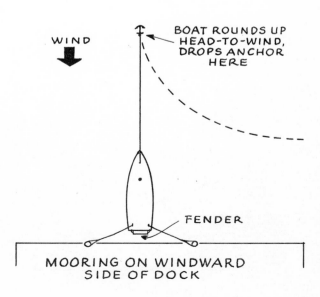

MOORING ON WINDWARD SIDE OF DOCK

wind, a comfortable distance off, and drop your anchor. Then pay out the anchor line until the stern is a few feet from the face of the dock. *Make certain* the anchor is dug in properly and is not dragging. Then secure the two stern lines as shown. This can only be considered a *temporary* mooring, for a short period, since there is always the possibility of the anchor dragging, and if this should happen, "crunch" —no boat! Furthermore, if there is a shift in wind direction, the boat will veer off one way or the other, and could foul a nearby boat, and could conceivably break out the anchor. So never leave the boat unattended when moored in this fashion.

The next diagram shows the proper method of mooring in a slip. Notice that the stern lines are led *along* the dock or bulkhead, rather than parallel to the boat's heading. This is to prevent the stern from swinging to port or starboard. The spring lines keep it from hitting the bulkhead. A fender over the transom is an additional precaution.

In theory, the bow lines keep the boat centered between the posts or piles, and

this they will do, providing the piles are nearly abreast of the bow of the boat. But sometimes, particularly if your boat is over 25 feet in length, you'll find the bow projects so far out from the piles that the bow lines lead at an acute angle. In this event, the boat will swing over and ride against one of the piles. The solution is to secure the bow lines to the *mast,* rather than to the mooring cleat on the forward deck.

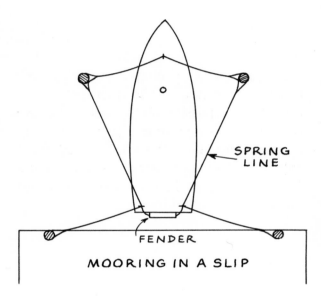

SPRING LINE

FENDER

MOORING IN A SLIP

Chapter 11

ANCHORING

Ground Tackle and Techniques

There are two requirements to be met in anchoring with safety—the anchor must dig in and hold without dragging or moving under the maximum strain of wind, sea and tide, yet can be freed and taken on board at will. Whether these requirements are met is determined by a number of factors: the nature of the bottom, the type and weight of the anchor, the length of the anchor line or "rode," and the weight of the boat. Hard and fast rules cannot be laid down to fit all conditions, since conditions vary with every anchorage, and no two boats are alike. The best we can do is to explain the basic principles and techniques, and with experience you judge what is best for your specific needs.

What Type of Anchor?

The most popular anchors currently in use are the *Yachtsman,* the *Danforth,* the *Northill,* and the "plow," or *C. Q. R.* No one of these can be called the "best," although each has its ardent proponents. Any one of them will hold your boat safely, *provided* it is of appropriate

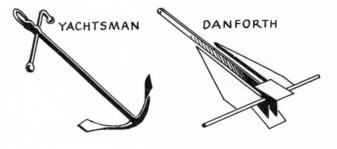

weight, has sufficient scope, and is firmly dug in. The manufacturers will supply tables showing recommended weights for various sizes and types of boats.

The *Yachtsman,* or Herreshoff-pattern anchor, is the easiest to set and best-holding in most varieties of bottom, particularly where the bottom is rocky. On the debit side, it will weigh two or three times as much as the other three, lightweight, types *for the same holding power.* It is also more awkward to handle and to stow.

The *Danforth* is *probably* the most popular type, although this is subject to debate. The reason it is preferred by those who favor it is that it stows easily. It lies flat on the deck and is less of a hazard to toes and shins.

The *Northill* stows nearly as well as the *Danforth,* since the stock is removable. The flukes stand on edge when the anchor is laid on deck, which some consider undesirable.

The *C. Q. R.* is called a "plow" because that is what it resembles. It is an awkward shape to be carried on deck, but most users get around that by carrying it in the bow chocks or lashed under the bowsprit, if there is one.

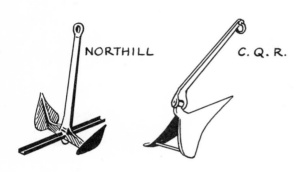

All types of anchors of proper weight can be made to hold if they are firmly dug into something solid, such as hard sand or clay. But where the bottom is covered with soft mud or silt and/or seaweed, kelp, or grass, the lightweight types sometimes fail to bite through to anything solid beneath. The flukes become "shod" with a big glob of mud or grass and, with a rising wind or sea, slowly but surely the anchor starts to drag.

The author lay one stormy night with his Danforth down in a mud bottom, without dragging, and in the morning it took a full hour of hard work to get it up. It seemingly had worked down halfway to China. During another memorable night, that same anchor dragged an eighth of a mile through a species of kelp known locally as "sea lettuce."

Always consult your chart before anchoring. The nature of the bottom is indicated by symbols: hard sand, rocky, mud, etc. You can't anchor safely without knowing the kind of bottom. Knowing this, you can estimate the amount of scope needed for the type of anchor used.

What Type of Anchor Line?

Before the advent of synthetics, manila rope was universally preferred for anchor rodes. Unfortunately, it has a short life—it rots easily and does not resist abrasion when wet.

Today, nylon is considered superior to any other kind of material for anchor lines. While its initial cost is higher than that of manila, it has a far longer useful life. Its main advantage for anchor lines is its amazing elasticity. As a boat surges back from the forces of wind and sea, a nylon line stretches like a spring, and the shock is dampened. Its strength is almost double that of manila, for a given size.

Nylon is seemingly impervious to mildew and rot, and can be stowed away wet without deterioration. Its only apparent enemy is that common to all fibers, chafe and abrasion—and simple preventive measures can take care of that.

How Much Scope?

The length of the anchor line between the boat and the anchor is called the *scope,* and it is primarily determined by the depth of the water. While conditions and boats may vary, a good average scope would be 6 to 1. This means that if you anchor in 10 feet of water, the scope should be 60 feet. But the *total length* of your anchor line should be at least a third more, since you must have extra line on deck for anchoring in deeper water, or in bad weather when you need more scope.

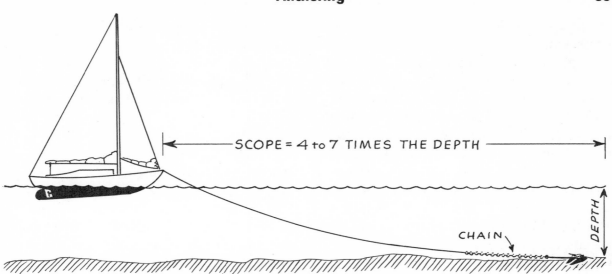

SCOPE = 4 to 7 TIMES THE DEPTH

DEPTH

CHAIN

The more nearly horizontal the pull on an anchor, the better it will hold. Note in the illustration that the catenary (or curve) of the line results in a horizontal pull at the anchor stock. This is an ideal situation. However, when the boat pitches in heavy seas, the line is lifted by the bow each time it comes up, and the pull on the shank is upward. The repeated movement with each lift eventually loosens the anchor's hold, and the boat will drag.

There are two ways to prevent an upward pull on the shank of the anchor—increase the amount of scope, or add weight to the line. Adding weight is the best preventative, and is easily done. Simply add a short length of galvanized chain, between the end of your line and the anchor. Thus, the weight is next to the shank and holds it down. For a boat around 25 feet, a 6-foot length of ¼-inch chain shackled to the shank will do the trick.

Preventing Chafe

In anything but a flat calm, an anchored boat is constantly moving, alternately pull-

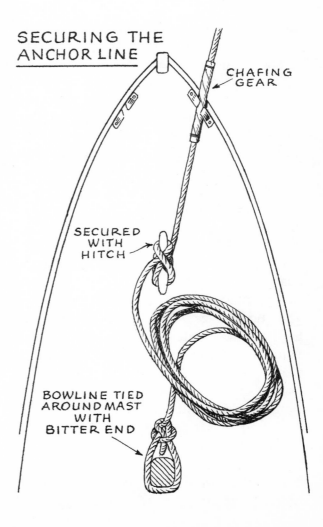

SECURING THE ANCHOR LINE

CHAFING GEAR

SECURED WITH HITCH

BOWLINE TIED AROUND MAST WITH BITTER END

ing and slackening the anchor line. If unprotected, the line chafes where it passes through the chock, and over a period of time, can saw completely through the line. *Always* apply chafing gear at that point. The simplest way is to wrap a strap of canvas spirally around the line for a foot or so where it rides in the chock, seizing the wrapping at each end with marline. An 18-inch piece of ordinary garden hose can be used, if it is slit lengthwise and seized at each end. There is available at marine stores a manufactured item called "chafe guard," which is a split sleeve of neoprene, complete with seizings at each end.

Choosing a Place to Anchor

The main considerations in anchoring safely are protection from sea or ground swell, shelter from prevailing or anticipated winds, and good holding ground. You must also know the depth of water, and the range of tide. If your boat's draft is 3 feet, and you anchor in 6 feet of water at flood tide where the range of tide is 4 feet, you'll be hard and fast aground at low tide.

Before anchoring in a strange harbor, consult the chart. Symbols shown on the chart will tell the nature of the bottom—sandy, muddy, rocky, etc. Reference to your tide tables will tell you the times of high and low water, and the range, which you must know to determine how much scope you need. As an example, in a harbor on the New England coast where the range, or rise and fall, is 10 feet, a boat anchored in 10 feet at *low water* with a scope ratio of 6 to 1 would have only a 3 to 1 scope at *high water*.

Another important consideration is having enough room to swing. The wind may change direction completely around the compass, and your boat is going to swing with it. If other boats are anchored near by, allow yourself enough room to swing clear of them if the wind shifts.

Getting the Anchor Down

The novice always throws or "heaves" the anchor clear of the boat. The seaman *lowers* it. The mechanics of anchoring are simple, but important.

Bring the boat up into the wind so that she comes to a dead stop with her bow right over the exact spot you have chosen. As she starts to drift back, your crew lowers the anchor to the bottom, paying out line through his hands. Immediately afterward, he puts a slight strain on the line as he pays it out. This slight but continuous strain starts the anchor digging in. When the required scope has been eased out, he *snubs* the line, by taking a quick turn on the mooring cleat or bit.

If the anchor is properly dug in, the boat is brought to a stop head to wind. If

TAKING A BEARING ON SHORE TO FIX ANCHORING POSITION

the anchor is dragging, the drag is often revealed by a slight tremor in the line as it is held in the hand. This is not infallible. With experience you can "sense" a dragging anchor.

When your crew is satisfied the anchor is holding, and has made the line fast, the next step is to take bearings on shore im-mediately. Sighting directly abeam, you notice a tree on shore that is in line with a chimney inland. As a good seaman, you will check periodically to see if they are *still* in line. If they separate, or start moving either way, you are positively dragging, and the quicker you get your hook up and re-anchor the better.

Chapter 12

THE RIGGING

The beginner with his first sailboat is often bewildered by the complex system of shrouds, stays, halyards, and sheets. He assumes they are all necessary, but may not know why. He can accept them as they are, and enjoy his sailing without unduly worrying about them. But when the day comes that he has to step, rig, and tune up the mast and rigging himself, he had better know what he is doing. Explained here are the basic principles of rigging, and how they affect the performance of a boat under sail.

Standing Rigging

Masts are held in place by shrouds and stays—shrouds take the side, or athwartship strains, and stays hold the mast in a fore-and-aft position. The number and placement of shrouds and stays depend on the size of the boat, and the customary practices of the designer. A 14-foot day sailer may have a single pair of shrouds and a jibstay, while a 40-footer would require a multiple system of shrouds and stays. To show the innumerable methods of staying a mast is impossible. Therefore, I have illustrated a common arrangement that might be employed on boats from 18 to 25 feet. Your own boat may or may not be rigged in a similar manner, but the basic elements will apply, and should be of help however it is rigged.

You will notice there are two sets of shrouds, upper and lower. The upper shroud supports the upper part of the mast, and goes over the spreader. When under sail, the strain on the windward upper shroud exerts a thrust or force against the mast at the point where the spreader is attached to it. To offset this force, the lower shroud takes part of the strain, since it is attached at the same point. Thus the spar and the upper and lower shroud form the familiar truss.

A mast, since it bears a great compression strain, must be kept *straight*, leaning neither to starboard nor port. If the upper shroud is looser than the lower shroud, the head of the mast will sag off to leeward, when under sail. If the lower shroud is too loose, the mast will be bowed. The mast must be plumb with the boat. This can be checked with a plumb bob, hung from the masthead by the main halyard. Obviously the boat must be at rest in quiet water, and level athwartship.

How much tension there should be on the shrouds is a moot question. The shrouds should not be so tight you can

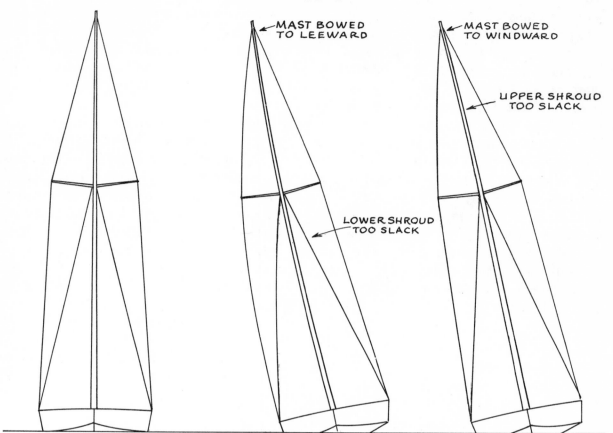

play a tune on them, nor so loose you can tie a knot in them, but something in between. Perhaps *taut,* but not *tight,* is the answer. One way to check is to go for a sail. When hard on the wind, the leeward shrouds should be definitely *slack.* If they are not, all shrouds must be slacked off a bit more.

In the fore and aft aspect, you probably have a jibstay, jumper stays, and a permanent backstay. The fore and aft position of the mast will vary with the designer. Some masts have a slight rake aft; generally, however, the mast is vertical. Under sail, hard on the wind, the pressure on the mainsail pulls the masthead aft. At the same time, below the masthead, the jib is pulling the mast forward, at the point where the jibstay is attached. The problem is to counteract these opposing forces.

On the foreside of the mast at the jibstay attachment, we have a light V-shaped affair called the *jumper strut.* The jumper stays are attached to the masthead, led over the strut, and returned to the mast below. They form a truss, the thrust of the strut against the mast offsetting the forward pull of the jibstay.

At the same time the jumper strut counteracts the pull aft exerted by the mainsail, on the masthead. But while we have managed to keep the upper part of the mast straight, the pressure of the jibstay is pulling the *entire* mast forward. To offset this, we put a permanent backstay on, from the masthead to the transom.

It should be apparent that the jibstay, jumpers, and backstay are vitally interrelated, and the tension of any one is dependent on the tension on the other two. Tighten the permanent backstay and you tighten the other two, and vice versa.

Stainless steel rigging wire has a certain amount of stretch. Therefore, when tuning up, it is common practice to have sufficient tension on the jumper stays to bow the mast forward *slightly*. When under sail, the greater tension of the jibstay being pulled forward by the jib will tend to straighten the mast out.

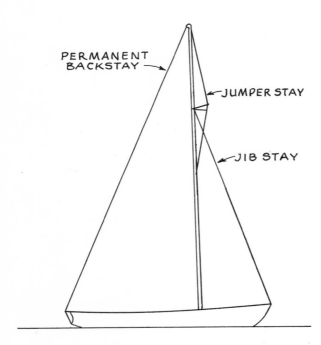

PERMANENT BACKSTAY
JUMPER STAY
JIB STAY

The final test for a properly tuned mast comes when you are under sail. Sight up the mast when you are sailing on various headings and see whether it is straight or not. If not, you should correct it.

Modern racing boats have many adjustments that can be made to the sails and the rigging. These adjustments are used to change the shape of the sails—which eliminates the need for many different sails for different conditions. The easiest way to change the shape of a mainsail is to bend the mast. (More on this in Chapter 13.) Taking up on the backstay bows the mast aft; therefore, many racing boats carry relatively slack jumpers and have means for quickly adjusting backstay tension. Mast jacks are also used in some boats to push the mast forward at the deck.

Some classes, such as the Laser, do not have standing rigging, but rely instead on hefty spar sections to keep the mast up. The Laser's mast will bend—sagging off both to leeward and aft—as will all unstayed spars. Control of aft bend is accomplished with the mainsheet and traveler. By adjusting them, you control the shape of the sail.

A masthead rig, where the jibstay is taken up to the masthead instead of only part way, has no jumpers and is less easily bent than other rigs. The backstay is often adjustable, but its function is only to tighten the jibstay. Since there are large compression loads on a masthead rig, it should be kept straight to keep the mast from getting out of column. Bent, the mast loses its ability to withstand compression.

Running Rigging

Here we are concerned with sheets and, to a minor degree, halyards. The best sheets are Dacron, either common 3-strand rope, or braided, which is the finest and most expensive. Halyards are flexible stainless steel, with a rope "tail," or hauling part.

Let's start with the jib sheets. They can

be single or double. If single, two sheets are spliced into the clew of the jib—one trims on the port side, the other on the starboard. Each is led through a block or fairlead on deck, and then aft to the cleat. If double, each sheet is fastened, or "dead-ended" on the deck, goes through a block shackled to the clew, back to a deck-block as before, and then aft. Thus you achieve a "purchase," with the power of two. This means that with double sheets it takes only half as much "beef" to trim the jib as it would with single sheets.

The big problem with jib sheets is deciding where to set the sheet leads—or to put it another way, how far out from the centerline of the boat, and how far aft from the clew of the jib the sheets should be trimmed. This is a moot question on which experienced skippers often disagree. The majority are generally agreed, however, on the ideal *thwartship* position, which is known as the "18-degree" line. The jib is trimmed at some point on a line running from the tack of the jib at an angle of 18 degrees from the centerline of the boat. The illustration shows how this line is laid out.

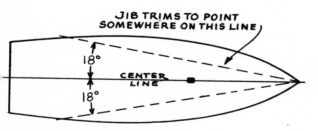

the deck. Now measure out on each side of the centerline, and perpendicular to it, 9 inches, and make a mark at these two points.

Now if you run a line from the jibstay point through these marks, extending them all the way to the edge of the deck, you'll have two lines that are each at an 18-degree angle with the centerline. *Somewhere* along each line is the point to which the jib sheet should be trimmed. You will want to move that point forward or aft to suit various winds and headings. Therefore it is customary to install a length of track on the line, on which the sheet-block can be slid forward or aft.

Look now at the profile drawing for the best *fore-and-aft* position of the blocks.

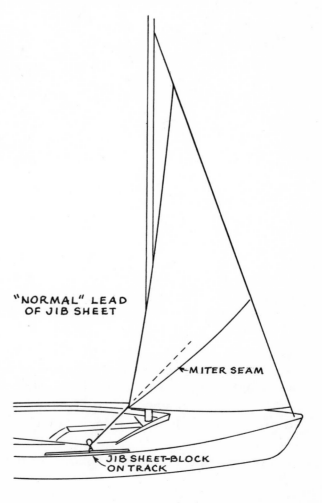

Stretch a length of twine along the deck, from the center of the forward side of the mast to the point of attachment of the jibstay. Be sure this is on the exact centerline of the boat. Measure back 5 feet from the jibstay and put a pencil mark on

The angle of lead will vary with every jib, and different boats. Some skippers insist the sheet should trim on a line with the miter seam of the sail, others say a little forward, or a little aft. In my opinion, you should install a 2-foot length of track so that the center is on a line with the miter, and thus you can shift the sheet block 11 inches forward or aft.

The best way to determine what is best for *your* jib is to go for a sail and see how the jib acts. Sail as close to the wind as possible, and start to luff up *very gradually*. Observe carefully where the jib luffs, or "breaks," first—the point on the luff where the first tremor or flutter appears.

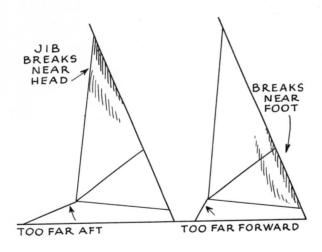

If the lead of the jib sheet is right, that point will be just a little above the intersection of the miter seam and the wire luff. If it appears much higher, move the sheet-block forward, if too low, move it aft. These are but general methods, and you work out your problems by trial and error.

If you have double jib sheets, the 18-degree rule still holds. In this case, a line *bisecting the two parts of the sheet* should fall on the 18-degree line, as shown in the illustration.

The jib sheet block is moved forward or aft to suit different wind conditions, and various headings. This is most important in racing, to get the best possible speed.

When you are sailing to windward in very heavy wind, the jib should be trimmed in hard, for that is when it should be as flat as possible. The force of the wind puts more tension on the sailcloth and the sheet, and there's more stretch in both. Thus it takes a lot of beef on the jib sheet to flatten the jib.

Mainsheet arrangements are of infinite variety, from the single sheet of a sailing pram that you hold in your hand to the six-part, multiple-block rig of a 12-meter that is trimmed by geared winches. Some have the mainsheet blocks bolted to the deck on the centerline, others straddle it, while on the majority of boats the block slides on a traveler or thwartship track.

But we are less concerned here with the mechanical arrangement of the mainsheet than the principles involved in trimming the mainsail for greatest efficiency.

As your eye travels aloft, you'll note that the sail has a twist, the upper part falling off away from the wind. The lower part, nearest the boom, is at a greater angle to the wind than the head of the sail. Ideally, the angle should be the same from the foot to the head, but this is not possible. As you can readily understand, with the head of the sail sagging off, there is less sail area working for you efficiently. This can be partially controlled by the lead, or direction of pull, of the mainsheet in relation to the centerline of the boat. (We are concerned here with sailing to windward, close-hauled.)

It is obvious that a *pull downward* on the boom tends to flatten the sail. The weight of the boom and its hardware, to a minor degree, contributes to a down-

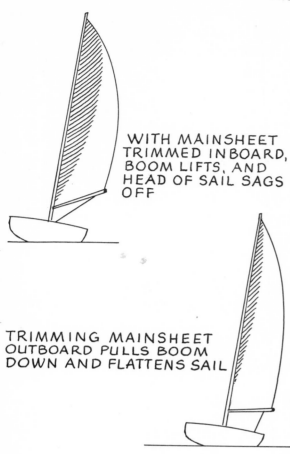

WITH MAINSHEET
TRIMMED INBOARD,
BOOM LIFTS, AND
HEAD OF SAIL SAGS
OFF

TRIMMING MAINSHEET
OUTBOARD PULLS BOOM
DOWN AND FLATTENS SAIL

is more *downward,* and if over-trimmed, the end of the boom drops down, which in turn tightens the leach and traps "dead air" in the sail.

There's a simple way to find out if you are trimmed too hard. With your eye on the boom end, ease the sheet out cautiously, *no more than an inch or two.* If the end of the boom *rises vertically,* it is trimmed too flat. Ease it out another inch, and if it starts to travel *out,* rather than *in,* STOP. This is the correct trim.

When close-hauled in very light winds, the mainsail cannot be sheeted in so flat, for it will kill the boat's speed, and you'll feel a lack of sensitiveness in the tiller. Just how much the sheet must be eased out is a point that can be determined by experience and constant observation, and will vary with different boats.

When sailing on a reach in light airs, the situation changes. Here you want more draft in the sail than when close-hauled. Easing off the clew outhaul helps some, and moving the sheet block *inward,* toward the centerline, gives a lift to the boom.

Earlier we spoke of the "twist," or sagging off of the sail in its upper part, and consequent loss of effective sail area. On a reach, this results in a considerable loss of speed. This is important, not only because of loss of speed but also because a twisting mainsail can induce rhythmic rolling or a capsize when running before the wind. The lead of the mainsheet is of no help, since the pull is *in* rather than *down.* Hanging a bucket of water on the end of the boom would be effective, but impractical. (We once saw two fourteen-year-olds win a race with this unorthodox brainstorm.)

ward pull. Therefore, moving the sheet block *outward* gives a more direct downward pull than if it were nearer the centerline, and the head of the sail sags off less. The majority of racing boats are fitted with track so that the position of the sheet block can be moved to various positions during the race, to adjust the lead for greatest efficiency.

The basic rule in trimming the mainsail for windward work, therefore, is *out-and-down.* There is one point, however, that many skippers either ignore or are not familiar with. When strapped down, hard on the wind, it is very easy to trim the sail *too flat* inadvertently, and it has no "lift." As the boom is trimmed in from a reaching position to a beat, the pull of the sheet

Most racing boats today control this sagging off by means of a rig called a *boom-vang,* often termed a *kicking-strap,* or *boom-jack.* As the illustration shows, it is simply a tackle attached to the boom and foot of the mast, which prevents the boom from lifting on a reach or run. A length of rubber shock cord acts as a retriever, to pull the tackle back out of the way when not in use. You should be warned that the boom-vang puts a terrific strain on the boom, gooseneck fitting, and mast. Therefore it should be designed and fitted only by someone experienced in its use.

The general procedure in setting the boom-vang is as follows: just before rounding the weather mark, where you'll be going from a beat to a run, the vang is set up hard, while the boom is still low and sheeted in hard. As the mainsheet is paid out, the boom cannot lift, as it normally would, and the sail will not sag off near the head. If you were to wait until you had rounded the mark and eased out the mainsheet, it would be difficult to set up the boom-vang, unless the wind were very light.

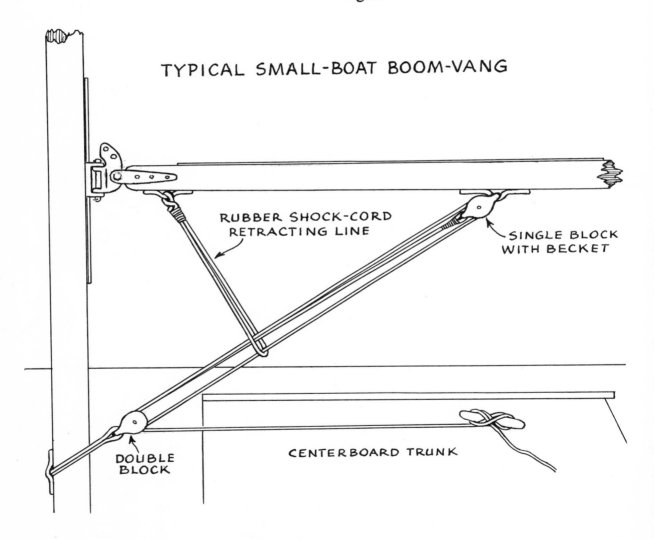

TYPICAL SMALL-BOAT BOOM-VANG

RUBBER SHOCK-CORD RETRACTING LINE

SINGLE BLOCK WITH BECKET

DOUBLE BLOCK

CENTERBOARD TRUNK

Chapter 13

THE SAILS: MAINSAIL AND JIB

Since the introduction of synthetic sailcloth, the art of sailmaking has become increasingly scientific.

The cotton sailcloth of former years had many shortcomings. It stretched considerably under strain, and once stretched, would not recover. When wet it shrank, was attacked by mildew, and quickly lost its strength. The stretch factor was unpredictable, and could not be measured. The sailmaker had to allow for this stretch in cutting a sail, and he had nothing to guide him except past experience. A new sail had to be broken in carefully, and a heavy-handed, careless sailor could utterly destroy its shape right at the start.

Thanks to Dacron, these problems are no longer a factor, and cotton sails are obsolete. Dacron has superb stability. Its fibers are water-repellent, the cloth doesn't shrink with increased humidity, and it is not attacked by mildew and rot.

Dacron has a certain amount of *elasticity,* which is not the same as stretch. Like an elastic band, it will elongate under tension, but return to its original dimension when tension is removed. Thus, the sailmaker can cut and sew a Dacron sail to a predetermined, measurable shape, with close tolerances. He knows that the finished sail will set exactly as he had planned. Because of its stability, a Dacron sail requires no breaking in—it takes its designed shape the first time it is set on the boat.

The Mainsail

The ideal shape of a sail, in cross section, is similar to that of a bird's wing, or an airfoil. The depth of this curve is called the *draft,* or "belly."

Ideally, for light winds a sail should have considerable draft, and for heavy winds much less. Topflight racing boats therefore have several ways to adjust draft, to meet different weather conditions. In a well-designed sail, the curvature is most pronounced in the forward part, the point of deepest draft being about a third of the distance from the luff, flattening out to a straight line as it approaches the leach.

The sailmaker builds the desired amount of draft into the sail in several ways—by shaping the edges on the luff and the foot, by varying the overlap of the individual cloths as he sews them together, and by the manner in which he sews on the roping.

Sailmaker roping a sail. Roping provides greatest strength plus resilience. (Courtesy Hard Sails, Inc.)

Note, in the line drawing, that the luff and the foot of the sail are not cut on a straight line, but on a gentle curve. When the sail is bent on the straight mast and boom, the excess cloth disappears in the designed draft. When a sail is designed for a "bendy" spar (see Chapter 12), the sailmaker gives it the maximum draft. Then, when the spar is bent to curve forward in the middle, the excess draft is removed from the sail. This allows the same sail to be used in both light air

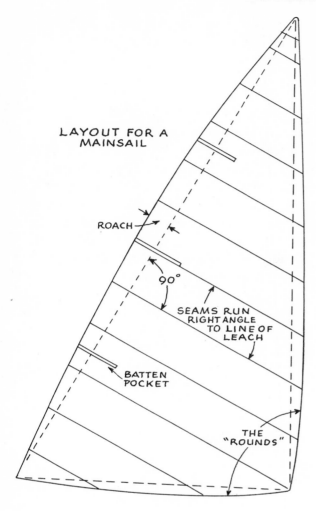

LAYOUT FOR A MAINSAIL

ROACH

90°

SEAMS RUN RIGHT ANGLE TO LINE OF LEACH

BATTEN POCKET

THE "ROUNDS"

the smooth, uninterrupted flow of air along the after part of the sail.

Be certain that the battens are the right length. They should fit snugly in the pockets.

The Jib

The jib is cut straight on the foot and on the leach, the exception being in the Genoa, or overlapping jib. Here the leach is generally "scooped," or curved reversely, so that the lee shrouds do not interfere with the natural set of the leach.

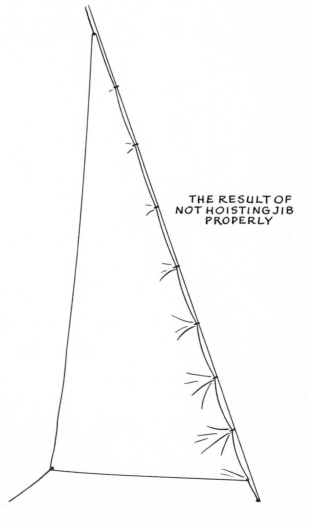

THE RESULT OF NOT HOISTING JIB PROPERLY

(straight mast, full sail) and heavy winds (bent mast, flat sail). Theoretically, this works as well with a bendy boom, but in practice it doesn't seem worth the bother.

The curvature of the leach is called the *roach*. Since the dimensions of a sail are limited by the spars, the sail area can be increased at the leach. In the rules of the one-design racing classes, the amount of roach is limited. To keep the excess cloth in the roach from falling off behind the sail, battens are required to extend the leach. It is of utmost importance that the leach be as flat as possible, to insure

The luff of the jib must be tight and straight, and pulled up taut so that there is a little slack in the jibstay. If the jib is *not* set up enough, the luff will "droop" between the jib snap hooks, increasingly nearer the tack, as shown in the illustration. This is decidedly sloppy seamanship, and the jib can't do the work for which it was intended.

Although working sails are made of Dacron, sailmakers use nylon—because of its lighter weight—for spinnakers.

Care of Sails

Your Dacron sails will not mildew, and they will have a longer life than cotton sails, but they should be cared for intelligently. Be careful with cigarette or pipe —a live ash will instantly melt a hole in Dacron. Don't leave the sails bent all the time without sail covers—stow them below in their bags. Sunlight is injurious to nylon and Dacron. Dust and acids and soot from oil burners are always in the air and are natural enemies.

When furling or stowing sails on a very hot day, don't let perspiration from your arms come in contact with the Dacron. Laboratory tests have determined that this is injurious. At the end of the sailing season, hose your sails down with fresh water, let them dry, fold neatly, and stow in their bags. Stow them for the winter in a dry place, *away from heat.*

Always fold Dacron sails to prevent cracking of the filler resin used to seal the fibers of the fabric.

Chapter 14

THE SAILS: SPINNAKER

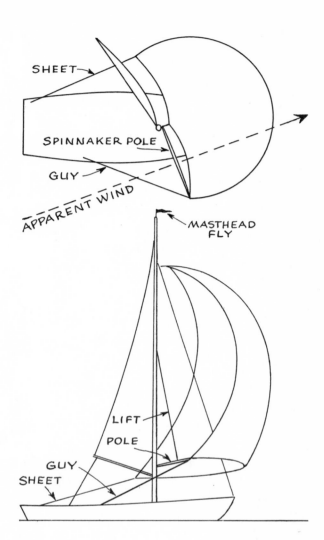

The spinnaker, sometimes referred to as the "parachute spinnaker," or "chute," is a semispherical sail of very light nylon used when running or on a broad reach. Its shape is an isosceles triangle whose base is the foot of the sail, controlled by a sheet attached to the leeward corner, and a guy attached to the weather, or windward corner. The sail billows out and upward over the bow, ahead of the jibstay, and is supported by the spinnaker pole, one end of which is attached to the mast, and the other to the weather corner, or tack. The weight of the pole is supported by a line called the *lift,* attached to the mast and the pole.

There are three cardinal rules to be observed in setting and trimming the spinnaker correctly, for maximum efficiency. First, the spinnaker pole must always be carried perpendicular, or at right angles, to the mast. Secondly, it must be trimmed square to the apparent wind, as indicated by the masthead fly. Thirdly, the foot of the sail must be parallel to the water, or horizon.

As shown in the illustration, the fitting on the end of the pole hooks into an eye on a slide, which runs on a track on the forward side of the mast. Thus the inboard

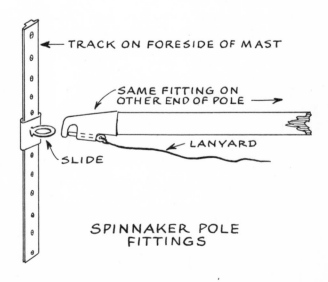

SPINNAKER POLE FITTINGS

end of the pole can be moved up or down when necessary, to keep the pole perpendicular to the mast.

While both sides of a spinnaker are identical, the weather, or windward edge is considered to be the luff, and the rest of the sail is trimmed as though it were a jib. As the sheet is let out, the luff begins to curl, and the spinnaker is on the point of collapsing. At this point the sheet must be trimmed in with a quick snap, or jerk, which will eliminate the curl. For a perfect setting spinnaker, the sheet is trimmed *just short of* the point where the luff begins to curl.

Preparing

The spinnaker can be set flying—but the cloth is so very light the slightest breath of air sets it in motion, and when hoisting it, folds of cloth can get wrapped around the shroud or jibstay, or become twisted and hopelessly fouled. It is common practice to prepare the sail in advance, preferably ashore, by folding or rolling it up in a certain manner, and *stopping* it. "Stopping" means tying *stops* of weak thread or rotten twine or rubber bands around the rolled-up sail at intervals along its length.

After the stopped sail is hoisted, a pull on the sheet breaks the stops successively, and the whole sail fills with wind instantly, without twisting or fouling. There are several methods of folding or rolling the sail for stopping, but the one shown here is the simplest, and most suitable for small boats.

The spinnaker is stretched out smoothly on the lawn, and one leach is carefully folded over to the other. Starting with the folded edge, the sail is tightly and evenly rolled up to the leaches. It takes two to do this properly—one pair of hands is not enough. You are now ready to tie on the stops, and the best stopping material is ⚹60 sewing cotton. The stops should be two to three feet apart. While your helper holds the rolled sail tightly, take three or four turns around it between his hands, and tie the thread securely.

When all the stops are tied, stretch the rolled sail out smoothly, without any twists, and with the two leaches straight along the roll. Now fold back and forth like an accordion, the folds two or three feet long, to form a neat bundle. Put a stop of four or five turns around the bundle, to keep it neat and in order until the time of setting.

Among some experienced racing skippers, stopping the spinnaker is considered unnecessary and outmoded. Instead, they fold the sail in a certain manner and stuff it into a bag, bucket, or box, leaving the three corners hanging out. The box is placed on deck, the halyard, sheet, and guy are attached, and the sail is hoisted speedily from the box in its folded position.

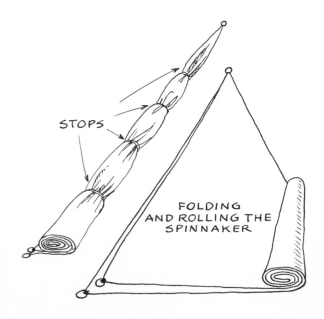

STOPS

FOLDING
AND ROLLING THE
SPINNAKER

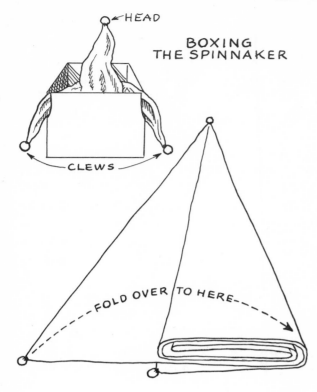

BOXING
THE SPINNAKER

HEAD

CLEWS

FOLD OVER TO HERE

and sheets attached. Pulling the halyard up sets the sail, then the crew connects the spinnaker pole. To douse the spinnaker, the halyard and sheets are let go and the sail is pulled back into the tube by a very light line that remains attached to the middle of the spinnaker. This system is quick and almost foolproof.

Most sailmakers make spinnaker "turtles" that are used in much the same way as a box. The turtle has a cover or tight mouth which keeps the sail contained until it is to be set. The sail may be stuffed hapazardly into the turtle as long as the luffs are kept separated and kept from twisting. The luffs, head, and clews go in last, and the three corners are left outside the turtle as with a box. Clips on the turtle allow it to be attached to the shrouds or special deck eyes to keep it from going over the side.

The diagrams show this method of folding. The sail is folded over with the top half extending about 18 inches beyond the edge of the underpart. Then the folded edge is folded over twice, and finally the extended edge is folded back over all. The sail now resembles a tube, and the two leaches are separated, and on opposite sides.

The sail is now flaked down, accordion-fashion, and stuffed in the box. The foot of the sail goes in first, with the two clews hanging out the corners of the box, and the head of the sail on top.

The simplest container is a square corrugated paper box. Two corners are slit partway down, and the clews are stuck through the slits.

Some racing boats, like the Fireball, have launching tubes built into the bow of the boat to house the spinnaker. The spinnaker lies inside the tube with halyard

Setting

Let us assume you are before the wind, on the starboard tack. The folded spinnaker is placed on the deck close to the mast, and on the side to *which the halyard leads*. Look aloft first to see on which side of the *jibstay* the spinnaker halyard leads. Assuming it is on the starboard side, the spinnaker is placed to starboard of the mast, and the halyard is snapped to the head of the sail. The halyard snap hook, by the way, should have a swivel, so that the stopped sail will not twist when hoisted.

The sheet is now attached, and must be led forward, around, and outside of the jibstay, then outside of the leeward shrouds and aft, where the skipper can hold it temporarily in his free hand. The guy is attached next, led outside the weather shrouds, and aft to the skipper. With the spinnaker pole close at hand, the crew

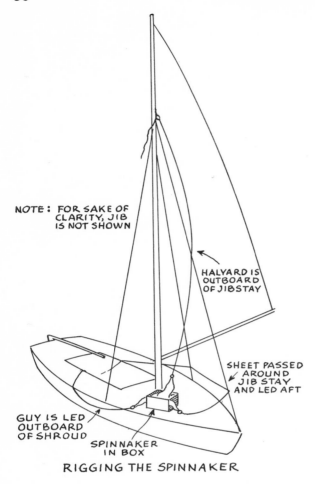

NOTE: FOR SAKE OF CLARITY, JIB IS NOT SHOWN

HALYARD IS OUTBOARD OF JIB STAY

SHEET PASSED AROUND JIB STAY AND LED AFT

GUY IS LED OUTBOARD OF SHROUD

SPINNAKER IN BOX

RIGGING THE SPINNAKER

the smaller boats, the spinnaker pole lift is often made of rubber shock cord, and requires little or no attention. Once the spinnaker is set and drawing, the jib is lowered and secured with a sail-stop to prevent it from getting overboard.

Spinnaker handling calls for long practice, perfect co-ordination between skipper and crew, and intense concentration every second, and the smaller the crew the more important these factors become. With a crew of three or four, each member can be allotted specific duties; they work as an interdependent team, and the skipper is free to concentrate on his steering.

In tending the spinnaker, the sheet is the critical factor. The sheet tender must never let his eyes stray a moment from the luff. The sheet must be constantly eased and trimmed to compensate for every slight shift of wind, "jerking" the sheet the moment the luff starts to curl. If the wind increases or slackens, the boat travels faster or slower, and the apparent-wind direction shifts accordingly. The spinnaker guy must be eased or trimmed to keep the pole square to the masthead fly at all times.

Jibing

The spinnaker can be jibed without collapsing or lowering it, and with no loss of valuable seconds on the downwind leg. When the skipper starts to jibe, and the mainsail starts over, unsnap the pole from the mast and snap it into the clew, so that both corners of the sail are attached to the pole. Pull the trip line which releases the pole from the tack, or weather corner of the sail. Then snap it into the mast fitting. With the boat now on the opposite tack, the former guy now becomes the sheet,

now quickly hoists the stopped sail, and snaps one end of the pole to *the ring in which he snapped the guy,* and snaps the other end to the mast fitting. A pull on the sheet and guy will now break out the spinnaker, as the stops break one by one and the wind opens it up.

With the skipper holding the sheet, the crew trims the guy in, looking aloft at the masthead fly, until the pole is at right angles to the apparent wind. As the skipper pulls in the sheet to the approximate point of proper trim, the crew sets the pole at the height at which it will be parallel to the horizon. He then steps aft and handles the sheet and guy from then on. On

1.
DETACH SPINNAKER
POLE FROM MAST

2.
SNAP POLE TO
OTHER CORNER
OF SAIL

3.
AS MAINSAIL JIBES,
RELEASE POLE FROM
OLD CORNER

4.
ATTACH POLE TO
MAST ON NEW
SIDE

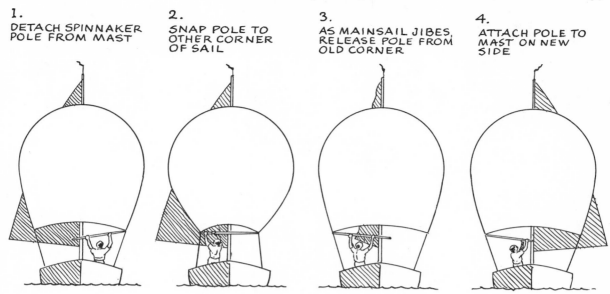

and the "old" sheet is the new guy. Both sheet and guy must now be trimmed to meet the "new" apparent-wind direction.

On the downwind run the weight should be aft, and the crew should never be on the forward deck oftener or longer than is absolutely necessary. In many boats, the spinnaker can be jibed from the forward end of the cockpit, without your having to get up on deck.

Dousing

In anything but the lightest breeze, getting the spinnaker in quickly and smoothly takes skillful handling, which only comes with practice. The one *big* danger is letting the sail get into the water. It could then drag under the boat, even take you with it, and result in a colossal foul-up.

The first step is to hoist the jib. The guy is slacked off, allowing the pole to swing around forward against the jibstay, and the spinnaker will swing around behind the mainsail where it will be blanketed, and will collapse. If the pole is *already* against the stay, because you are on a broad reach, the skipper should *bear off on a run* until the spinnaker is blanketed. The pole is now unsnapped, and the spinnaker is hauled in under the foot of the jib, while another crewman lowers the halyard. The sail is stuffed carefully in its bag or box, leaving the sheet, guy, and halyard attached, ready to be hoisted when needed.

THISTLES *on the move with spinnakers. (Photo by Mike Jahn)*

Getting ready for a race. (Photo by Mike Jahn)

Chapter 15

RACING

Before we get into the mechanics of racing, it is necessary to understand racing terminology and interpret it correctly.

Definitions

A boat that is racing *starts* when any part of her hull, crew, or equipment first crosses the starting line in the direction of the first mark of the course. She *finishes* when any part of her hull, crew, or equipment crosses the finish line from the direction of the last mark of the course.

The starting line is generally laid out at right angles to the first leg of the course, and all marks of the course are left (passed) on the same side. After the start, the committee boat shifts her position to the other side of the starting mark. This brings the finish line at right angles to the last leg of the course.

To *leeward* means on the side on which the boat is carrying her boom. To *windward* means the other side. These terms, under the rules, apply only to boats on the *same tack*. A boat is said to be *on a tack* except when she is in the act of coming about or jibing.

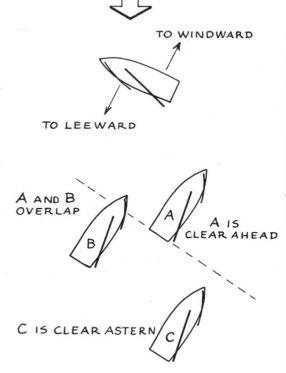

A boat is *clear astern* of another when her hull, spars, and sails are aft of a line projected abeam from the aftermost part of the other boat. The other boat is then said to be *clear ahead*. When neither boat is clear astern, or an intervening boat overlaps them both, they are said to *overlap*.

Luffing is altering course toward the wind, and *bearing away* is altering course away from the wind. In common usage, "bearing off" is the same as bearing away.

A *proper course* is any course you might sail after the start to complete the race as quickly as possible.

A *mark* is an object you are required to pass on a specified side. It marks the beginning, the boundary, or the end of a leg of the racing course.

An *obstruction* means a boat at anchor, under way, or aground, a pier, fish trap, or a reef or shoal over which you cannot safely pass. A yacht competing against you is also considered an obstruction, *providing she has the right-of-way*.

Right-of-Way Rules

In this country all yacht races are conducted under the rules set up by the North American Yacht Racing Union, and there are nearly seventy of them, with many parts to each. We propose to discuss here only those concerned with right-of-way,

THISTLES *racing. (Photo by Mike Jahn)*

since these are of most concern to the beginner. When a yacht violates a rule, she has committed a *foul,* and is automatically subject to disqualification. If the skipper *knows* he has committed a foul, he is required to drop out of the race immediately.

First, let us consider the rules that may apply *at any time.*

1. *On opposite tacks:* "A port-tack yacht shall keep clear of a starboard-tack yacht."

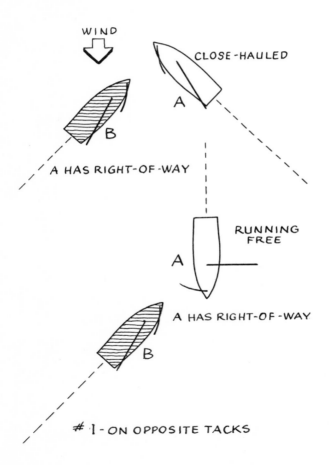

 # 1 – ON OPPOSITE TACKS

This means that if you are sailing on the port tack, and approaching a boat that is on the starboard tack, you must *keep out of her way.* This rule holds whether you are beating to windward, reaching, or running.

2. *On same tack:* "A windward yacht shall keep clear of a leeward yacht." Again, this applies whether you are beating, reach-

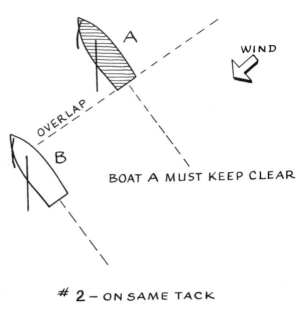

 # 2 – ON SAME TACK

ing, or running, but the two boats must be within two boat-lengths of each other, and they must *overlap.* If a line drawn across the bow of one boat would cross the other boat, then there is an overlap. Since the leeward boat has the right-of-way, she can alter course to windward, or "luff," and the windward boat must respond by doing the same until the mast of the leeward boat is abeam of the helmsman of the windward boat. There is an exception to the "same tack" rule. A boat establishing an overlap from clear astern of another boat on the same tack must keep clear.

3. *Passing marks on same or opposite tacks:* If boats overlap on reaching a mark which they are required to round and the overlap was established within two boat-lengths of the mark, the outside boat must give the inside boat sufficient room to round. This is referred as "buoy room."

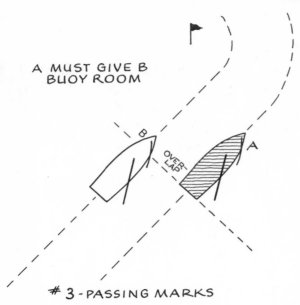

A MUST GIVE B
BUOY ROOM

3 - PASSING MARKS

4. *Tacking and jibing:* "A yacht while tacking or jibing shall keep clear of a yacht on a tack." This means you cannot tack or jibe directly in front of another boat in such a manner that she has to alter course to avoid a collision.

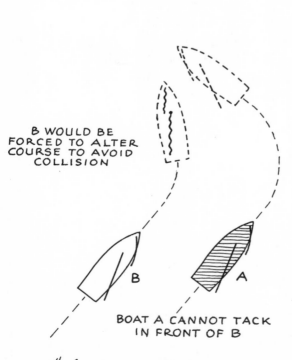

B WOULD BE
FORCED TO ALTER
COURSE TO AVOID
COLLISION

BOAT A CANNOT TACK
IN FRONT OF B

4 - TACKING AND JIBING

The following rules apply *only at the start*.

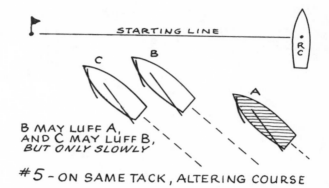

STARTING LINE

B MAY LUFF A,
AND C MAY LUFF B,
BUT ONLY SLOWLY

5 - ON SAME TACK, ALTERING COURSE

5. *On same tack, altering course:* Before starting, a *leeward* boat may alter course, but only *slowly*, if the change of course would affect another boat.

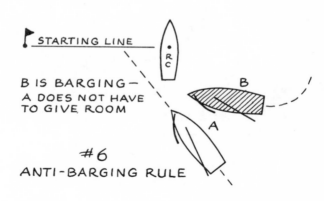

STARTING LINE

B IS BARGING—
A DOES NOT HAVE
TO GIVE ROOM

#6
ANTI-BARGING RULE

6. *On same tack, anti-barging rule:* When approaching the starting line, and about to start, a leeward boat does not have to give a windward boat room to pass between her and the starting mark, but she may not sail above her proper course after the starting signal to keep another from starting.

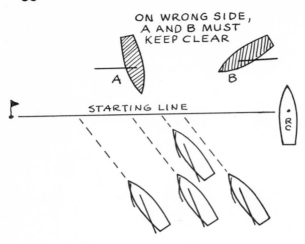

ON WRONG SIDE, A AND B MUST KEEP CLEAR

A   B

STARTING LINE

R C

#7 - ON WRONG SIDE OF STARTING LINE

7. *On same or opposite tacks, on wrong side of starting line at start signal:* A yacht on the wrong side of the signal, when her start signal is made, shall keep clear of all yachts that were on the right side. This means that if you are on the wrong side of the line, having crossed it before the starting gun goes, you must return and start properly. But you must keep clear of *all other boats* that *have* started properly. While returning to restart, you have no rights whatsoever.

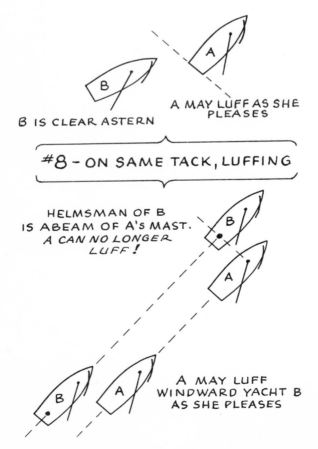

B IS CLEAR ASTERN

A MAY LUFF AS SHE PLEASES

#8 - ON SAME TACK, LUFFING

HELMSMAN OF B IS ABEAM OF A's MAST. A CAN NO LONGER LUFF!

A MAY LUFF WINDWARD YACHT B AS SHE PLEASES

After Starting

8. *On same tack, luffing:* After starting, a yacht may luff a yacht that is clear astern, or a windward yacht, as she pleases, and head to wind until the helmsman of the windward yacht comes abreast of the mainmast of the leeward yacht. The best way to understand this rule is to study the diagrams.

9. *On same tack, bearing away:* When sailing on a free leg of the course, a yacht shall not sail below her proper course when she is within three lengths of a leeward yacht, or of a yacht that is clear astern, and steering a course to pass to leeward. This means that when on a reach or when running, a boat must not bear off to prevent a leeward boat from passing. Or if a boat that is clear astern is steering a course to pass you to leeward, you cannot bear off to interfere.

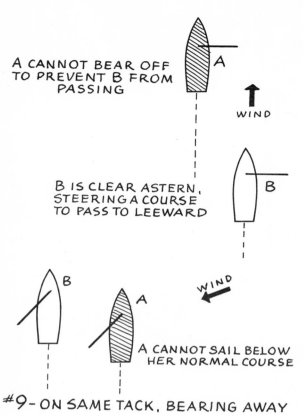

A CANNOT BEAR OFF TO PREVENT B FROM PASSING

B IS CLEAR ASTERN, STEERING A COURSE TO PASS TO LEEWARD

WIND

A CANNOT SAIL BELOW HER NORMAL COURSE

#9 - ON SAME TACK, BEARING AWAY

each boat has a handicap, generally expressed in seconds-per-mile. To each boat's elapsed time for the course, its handicap is applied, and the race results are determined by *corrected* times. Thus a boat that finishes third on elapsed time, could, by virtue of her handicap, win the race on corrected time.

Racing courses are generally triangular, windward-leeward, or a combination of both. The triangular course gives competitors a beat, reach, and run. The windward-leeward is just a beat and a run. As you sail around the course, all marks of the course are left or passed on the same side. If the course is to be sailed counterclockwise, all marks are left to port (this is most often the case). If clockwise, all marks are left to starboard.

The "Olympic Course" combines the triangular and windward-leeward courses

Avoiding Collisions

10. Under the proprieties of yacht racing, when a serious collision is imminent, all yachts involved must do their utmost to avoid it, *regardless* of any rule or right-of-way situation.

How Races Are Conducted

There are two kinds of racing—class racing and handicap racing. The first is for one-design boats; each class has its own starting time, but all sail the same course. Handicap racing is for boats that are dissimilar, such as cruising auxiliaries, and

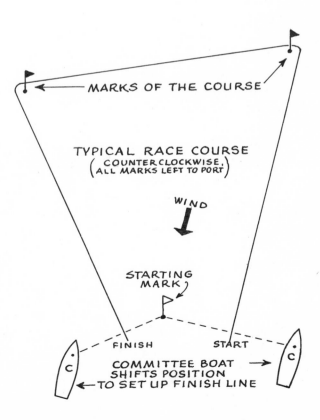

MARKS OF THE COURSE

TYPICAL RACE COURSE (COUNTERCLOCKWISE, ALL MARKS LEFT TO PORT)

WIND

STARTING MARK

FINISH   START

COMMITTEE BOAT → SHIFTS POSITION ← TO SET UP FINISH LINE

into a six-legged course. The first leg is to windward. The second and third legs are reaches (completing the triangle). The fourth leg is another beat to windward. The fifth leg is a run to the starting mark. The sixth leg is a third beat to windward with the finish line established at the windward mark. This course provides all points of sailing and maneuvers and is 50 percent windward work.

Marks of the course may vary with different clubs and localities. They may be a buoy, with or without a flag, a stake with flag, an oil drum painted a distinguishing color, or an anchored dinghy with a flag staff. If you or your crew or any part of your boat touches a mark of the course, you must reround the mark before continuing in the race.

The *starting line* is an imaginary line between the first mark of the course and the Race Committee boat, which is anchored. It is set at right angles to the first leg of the course, and is *usually* at right angles to the wind direction. (Sometimes the starting line is *not* at right angles to the wind. When this is the case, your starting tactics are altered to take advantage of it, as you shall see later.)

After the last boat has started, and the race is officially under way, the Committee boat ups anchor and moves around so that the finish line is at right angles to the last leg of the course.

The starting signals given by the Race Committee are visual and audible: a hoisted flag, cone, cylinder, or ball, which can be plainly seen, and a gun, whistle, or horn. Three signals are given for a start: *warning*, *preparatory*, and *start*. At exactly ten minutes before the start, a flag or "shape" goes up on the Committee boat, and a gun is fired simultaneously. This is the warning gun. The shape stays up exactly four and a half minutes, and then drops. By this, you know that another signal is coming in exactly thirty seconds.

Then, five minutes before the start, the flag or shape goes up and the gun is fired. This is the preparatory signal. After four and a half minutes the shape comes down, and thirty seconds later the gun is fired and a flag goes up, which means *start*. Since guns sometimes misfire, the flag marks the *official* start.

If you are to time your starts with any degree of accuracy, you should have a stopwatch—not just *any* stopwatch, but one designed expressly for yacht racing. A push on the stem at ten minutes-to-go, and it tells you *how much time remains* before the start, in minutes and seconds.

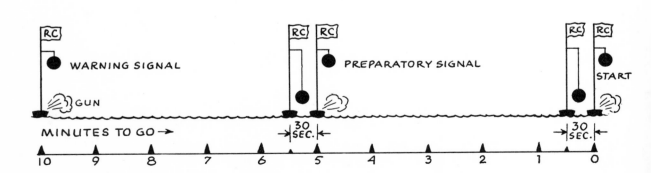

Racing Tactics

One of the secrets of winning races is *preparation,* attending to details that should be taken care of *before* the start. The following checklist covers most of these details, which are standard procedures with every successful racing skipper.

1. Before the race, get the race circular, or race instructions that describe the courses and rules to be followed, and *memorize* them. If there is any point you do not understand, ask someone who does. Be sure a copy is *aboard your boat,* for ready reference *during* the race. Be sure you know what and where the marks for all courses are, and whether you leave them to port or starboard.

2. Get the latest weather report for your area. Check the wind direction and force, and its relation to each leg of the course.

3. If you are in tidal waters, note the time of tidal change from the tide table. From your current table, note the time of current change, and the force and strength of current to be encountered during the race, and pencil it in on your chart of the course. Draw an arrow across the chart to show direction of current in relation to the race course.

4. Get out to the starting line early—at least a half-hour before start time.

5. Put your boat head-to-wind in the middle of the starting line, to determine which is the *favored end.*

6. Don't get very far away from the line during your starting period—if the wind drops, you could be becalmed or much too late reaching the line.

7. Practice the kind of start you plan to make, using the stopwatch.

The Start

The objective in starting is to be at the line just as the gun goes, sailing across in the proper direction, and *with full headway.* You must determine which end of the starting line is *nearer the* course to the next mark. Head your boat directly into the wind, on the middle of the line, and sight abeam in both directions. If either end of the line is noticeably to *windward* of your beamsight, that end is the *favored end.*

There are several methods of starting, only one of which can safely be recommended.

1. *Sitting on the line.* In this method, you sail up just short of the line, with a minute or so to go, and let your sails luff freely, waiting for the gun to go. Just before the gun you trim in your sheets and try to get under way. This takes considerable time, and your competitors are bearing down on you under full speed. You cannot get out of their way, or respect their rights, since you do not have way on, and therefore little control. This is a very poor starting approach, and the best advice is not to try it.

2. *Running the line.* This method is the favorite of beginners. You sail along the line, parallel and near to it, with half a minute or so to go, planning to trim sheets, head up, and cross the line at the gun. It sounds fine, but in the meantime, boats below you are heading for the line with full headway, close-hauled. Since you are the windward boat, they have the right-of-way. They can force you to head up into the wind and over the line *before* the gun goes, and then you are in trouble. The only time this may work is when you

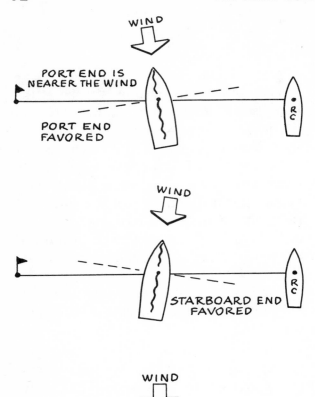

arrive at the line a *little* early and must use up fifteen or twenty seconds, while all the other boats are late, which may never happen.

3. *The timed start*. This is the most commonly used method. Basically, you pick the spot on the line where you want to cross, run away from the line a given number of seconds, allow the right amount of time for turning, then sail back to the line, close-hauled, for the same number of given seconds. The diagram shows the maneuver.

Timing is all-important; let your crew handle the stopwatch, calling out the seconds for each phase. Long before race time, you should have practiced reaching away from the line, coming about, and heading back close-hauled. The purpose of this is to determine exactly how many seconds it takes to turn about, from the reach to the beat. Next, sail close-hauled toward the desired spot on the line, and as you do so, look directly astern and line up some object on shore. This will be your

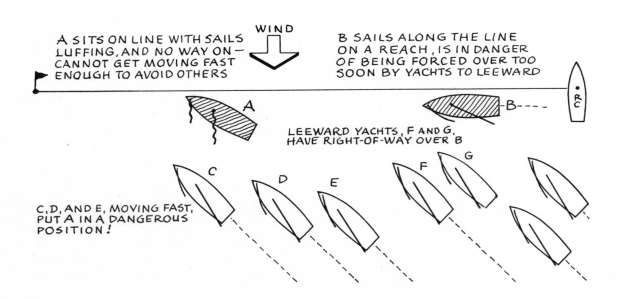

range marker, and by lining it up you are enabled to sail the same course from and toward the line. Now to put it to practice.

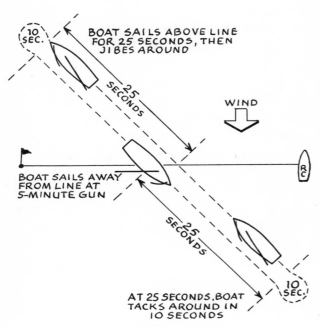

10 SEC. BOAT SAILS ABOVE LINE FOR 25 SECONDS, THEN JIBES AROUND

25 SECONDS

WIND

BOAT SAILS AWAY FROM LINE AT 5-MINUTE GUN

RC

25 SECONDS

AT 25 SECONDS, BOAT TACKS AROUND IN 10 SECONDS

10 SEC.

MULTIPLE PASS, TIMED START

At the preparatory gun (or five-minute gun) cross the line heading for your range marker, sail twenty-five seconds, turn about, head back to the line close-hauled, continue *above* the line for twenty-five seconds, then back to the line to start another run. The *times* I have given are only for demonstration; you work out your own. Small boats usually take 30 seconds to 1 minute to run away from and back to the line. A large cruising boat might use up to 2½ minutes.

COUNTING TIME FOR STARTS

Your crew must be alert for the warning signal, watch in hand. At the instant the signal is hoisted, or the smoke puff

from the gun is seen (whichever is first), the watch is started. Until the preparatory gun, your crew should call off the minutes remaining: "Nine minutes to go . . . eight minutes to go . . . seven minutes . . ." etc.

One-half minute before the next gun, he checks his watch as the signal comes down. If his timing is off, he should stop the watch and reset it when the preparatory signal is made. From now until the start, he calls the time more frequently. "Five minutes to go . . . four and a half to go . . . four minutes . . ." etc. With one minute to go, every five seconds. "Fifty-five, fifty, forty-five, forty," etc. until the last ten seconds, then "ten, nine, eight, seven, six, five, four, three, two, one, GUN!"

HOW TO START WITH NEITHER END OF THE LINE FAVORED

Here, since you have a choice that is fairly obvious, you should cross the line on the starboard tack, as close to the starboard end of the line as possible. You have the right-of-way over any boat starting on the port tack.

HOW TO START WITH STARBOARD END FAVORED

Race Committees try to avoid setting up a line of this type, since a traffic jam generally results. Everybody tries to cross on the starboard tack at the extreme starboard end of the line. In theory, this is the proper way to cross, *providing* you have the necessary skill, experience, and intestinal fortitude. But if you are a beginner, or the more conservative type, you would be well advised to start to leeward

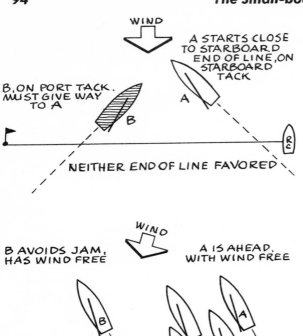

NEITHER END OF LINE FAVORED

WIND

A STARTS CLOSE TO STARBOARD END OF LINE, ON STARBOARD TACK

B, ON PORT TACK, MUST GIVE WAY TO A

of the jam, with full headway and more elbowroom. You might also start just behind A if you will want to sail on the port tack right after starting.

HOW TO START WITH PORT END FAVORED

Here the best start is at the port end, on the starboard tack. Since the port end is nearer the wind, you are thus already ahead of those who started in the middle or the starboard end. There is sometimes a situation where it is advisable to make a *port tack* start. *If* the port end of the line is *greatly* favored, and *if* there are few or no boats at that end of the line, a port tack start can pay off. However, you must have full headway, travel fast, and be prepared to give way to the other boats coming up on the starboard tack.

WIND

B AVOIDS JAM, HAS WIND FREE

A IS AHEAD, WITH WIND FREE

STARBOARD END FAVORED

The most important factor in starts is *speed*. Speed means control, the ability to alter course quickly with the least loss of time. Keep your boat footing all the time, and don't pinch. If you pinch (or try to sail too close to the wind), you kill your speed and are vulnerable to your competitors. So if you are close-hauled, ease the sheet a bit, bear off a little bit, and keep her moving fast. If you come up to the line too early, and boats are crowding you, it is better to go over with speed, then come back and restart, than to chance a collision trying to kill time with no way on.

WIND

A STARTS AT PORT END ON STARBOARD TACK, IS ALREADY AHEAD OF COMPETITORS

B AND C, ON PORT TACK, MUST GIVE WAY TO OTHERS

PORT END FAVORED

The Windward Leg

In beating to windward, always take the tack that puts you nearest the next mark. Tack as little as possible. Two long

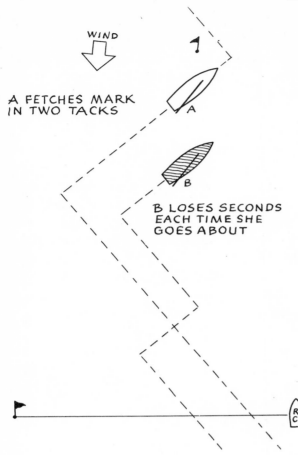

WIND

A FETCHES MARK
IN TWO TACKS

A

B

B LOSES SECONDS
EACH TIME SHE
GOES ABOUT

R
C

effective on a beat to windward. Its effect is to take all the drive and power out of the sails of the windward boat, and it cannot point as high.

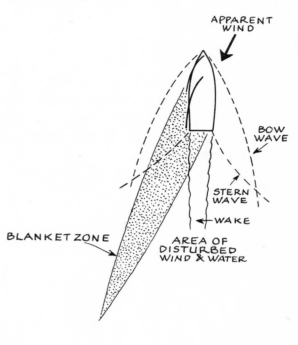

APPARENT
WIND

BOW
WAVE

STERN
WAVE

WAKE

BLANKET ZONE

AREA OF
DISTURBED
WIND & WATER

The most effective position for back-winding is to be close to leeward, and slightly ahead of another boat. This is called the *safe leeward position*. If you are

tacks are better than six short ones, since you lose valuable seconds each time you go about.

Other boats can affect your wind, by blanketing and by backwind. Blanketing is taking the wind from a boat that is to leeward. The blanket zone, or wind shadow, extends about six mast-lengths, varying with the strength of the wind, and seems to trail along in the direction of the *apparent* wind. If you get in the blanket zone of another boat, get out of it as quickly as you can, since you are sailing in "dead" air. Either change tacks, or fall off till you get your wind clear.

Backwind is the deflection of wind off the sails of another boat; the wind strikes the leeward side of the sails of your boat if it is to windward. Backwinding is most

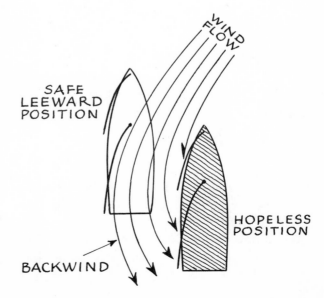

WIND
FLOW

SAFE
LEEWARD
POSITION

HOPELESS
POSITION

BACKWIND

doing the backwinding and are close enough to the windward boat, you can increase the deflection of the wind by trimming your mainsail in flat.

Passing

Never stay in the wake, the blanket zone, or the wind shadow of another boat. Passing to windward is very difficult, unless your boat can definitely point higher and foot faster. Sailing through to leeward is safer, but in either case, your boat must be well tuned and well sailed.

BY PINCHING AND SAILING HARD, A GAINS SAFE LEEWARD POSITION

WIND

A DRIVES OFF THROUGH TIP OF B'S WIND SHADOW

BREAKING THROUGH TO LEEWARD

A IS IN BAD POSITION

The technique in passing is to bear off a little and with increased speed run through the tip of the blanket zone of the other boat. Once clear of wake and backwind, you immediately sail hard, pinching a bit if need be, and make an intense

effort to work up to windward. You lose a little distance in this maneuver, but it can put you in the safe leeward position, where you can give the other boat a taste of backwind.

How to Plan Your Tacks

Your objective on the windward leg is to get to the mark in the shortest possible time, and when you reach it, to be in a position that gives you an advantage over other boats.

The windward leg is almost never perfectly square with the wind, and so the ideal tactic is to get there in one long tack

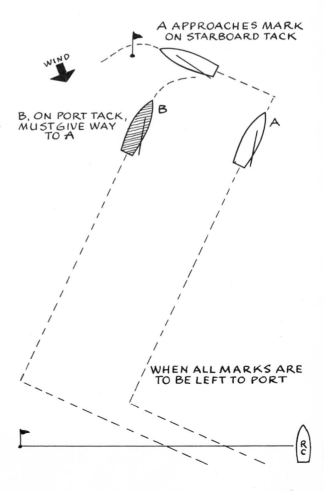

A APPROACHES MARK ON STARBOARD TACK

WIND

B, ON PORT TACK, MUST GIVE WAY TO A

B

A

WHEN ALL MARKS ARE TO BE LEFT TO PORT

R C

and a short one, arriving at the mark in a position to round it without tacking. Your first, long tack should be the one that takes you nearest the mark. If the wind shifts in your favor, you won't have wasted time sailing farther away from the mark. Furthermore, when it's time to come about, it is easier to judge when you can fetch the mark, since you are closer.

To tell when you can fetch the mark, sight directly across the boat, at right angles to your heading. When the mark is in this line, you should be able to fetch, or "lay" it. But your boat makes a certain amount of normal leeway; the wind may slacken or head you, and current can set you down to leeward. So carry on a bit farther before going about, to allow for these factors. Experience with your boat will help you to determine the best time to tack.

If the mark must be passed (or left) to port, you should fetch the mark on the starboard tack. You have the right-of-way, and can round without tacking. If the mark is to be passed to starboard, you should fetch it on the *port* tack. This sounds wrong, but if several boats are coming up on the mark on the port tack, and you are on starboard tack, *you cannot tack in front of them*. They merely bear off a bit, go under your stern, and round the mark ahead of you.

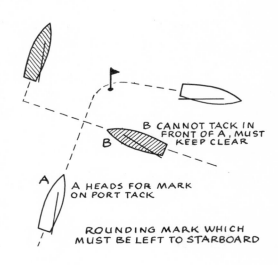

B CANNOT TACK IN FRONT OF A, MUST KEEP CLEAR

A HEADS FOR MARK ON PORT TACK

ROUNDING MARK WHICH MUST BE LEFT TO STARBOARD

Reaching

On the reaching leg, these are the points to remember: keep your wind clear, try to pass to leeward or well up to windward to avoid being luffed, and maneuver to be the inside boat at the leeward mark.

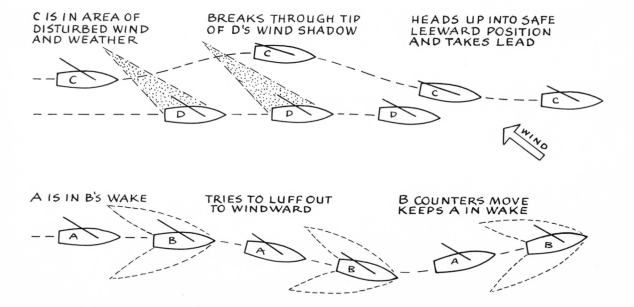

C IS IN AREA OF DISTURBED WIND AND WEATHER

BREAKS THROUGH TIP OF D'S WIND SHADOW

HEADS UP INTO SAFE LEEWARD POSITION AND TAKES LEAD

WIND

A IS IN B'S WAKE

TRIES TO LUFF OUT TO WINDWARD

B COUNTERS MOVE KEEPS A IN WAKE

Try to keep the boat astern of you in your zone of backwind and in your wake. Counter every *windward* move she makes, but you must not sail below your normal course to keep her from passing to leeward.

If the situation is reversed, and you are sailing in the disturbed water of a boat's wake, and influenced by her backwind, you must take the offensive and break through into the clear. To break through to windward, at a favorable moment trim sheets and luff to accelerate, and cut through at the exact intersection of the other boat's bow and stern waves, and you must pass her at least a mast's length to windward.

To break through to leeward, ease your boat off gradually to the tip of the other's wind shadow. Just before reaching it, trim sheets and head up at accelerated speed to break through the wind shadow, and then try to get the safe leeward position.

ROUNDING MARK WITH OTHERS

ROUNDING MARK ALONE

Rounding the Mark

Long before reaching the mark, you should plan to be the *inside* boat at the buoy, and sail the course accordingly. You should try to establish an overlap on the boat nearest you, so that you will be entitled to *buoy room*, and in addition, be the *windward* boat *after* you have rounded.

If you are alone, with no boats near you, be sure you round properly, as shown in the diagram, so that you lose no time or distance.

Before the Wind

Here, the most effective weapon is blanketing. The blanketing zone before the wind may extend four or more mast-lengths. When a boat comes up astern and blankets you, your only offense is to luff. But he luffs also, to keep you blanketed, and before you know it, you are luffing each other far off the course, losing valuable time and covering more miles than necessary. Sooner or later you both realize you must *finish* the race. Then you see that while you were engaged in this exciting but pointless duel, all the other boats were making a beeline for home, and are now far ahead. The moral is, don't get involved in a prolonged luffing match unless you need to beat the boat you are luffing in order to win a series of races and the other boats that could get ahead of you are not in contention for the series.

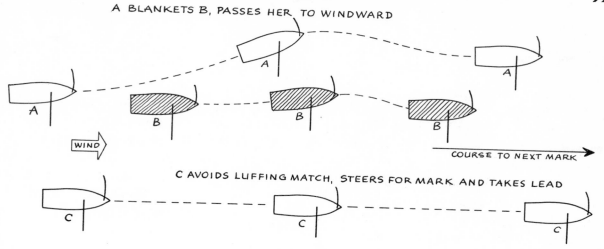

A BLANKETS B, PASSES HER TO WINDWARD

WIND

COURSE TO NEXT MARK

C AVOIDS LUFFING MATCH, STEERS FOR MARK AND TAKES LEAD

It is good tactics, if possible, to blanket the boat ahead, take her wind, and pass her to windward. But reserve this maneuver until you are well down the course. Otherwise, she can use the same tactic, swinging across your stern and blanketing you. Time it, therefore, so that you can cross the finish line immediately after you pass her.

If you are threatened by a boat close astern that is about to blanket you, *luff*. But luff so sharply that she cannot pass to windward. When you bear away, you'll still be ahead.

There is an advantage in staying to leeward on the downwind leg. There will be a natural tendency for most of the boats to edge out gradually to windward, high of the course, in order to keep their wind clear and blanket the next boat. If you see this happening, hold straight for the finish line, even bearing off a little and hardening up later. Thus you sail the shortest possible distance, keep your wind clear, and *may* be a winner.

One trick to make maximum speed downwind, if the wind is quite gusty, is to *bear off* in the puffs, and luff in the lulls.

This is, in effect, tacking downwind without jibing, keeping your boat sailing at maximum speed.

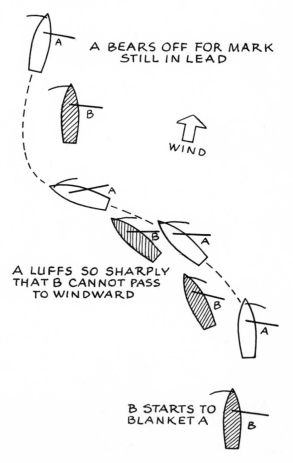

A BEARS OFF FOR MARK STILL IN LEAD

WIND

A LUFFS SO SHARPLY THAT B CANNOT PASS TO WINDWARD

B STARTS TO BLANKET A

Current Effects

No sailor worth his salt ignores currents, and nowhere is this more important than in racing, particularly in the beat to windward. A current running across the course can cause you to overstand the mark on the final tack, or set you down to leeward and force you to take an extra tack. Either way, you lose valuable time, and can lose any advantage you may have gained over your competitors.

It should be remembered that a current is going to carry the boat along with it, whether you like it or not, and speed *through the water* is not as important as speed *over the bottom*. If you are sailing through the water at 5 knots, and the current is flowing directly toward you at 2 knots, your speed over the bottom is only 3 knots. Conversely, with a 2-knot cur-

rent coming from astern, your speed over the bottom will be 7 knots.

Suppose you are sailing on a beam reach across a current that is running more or less with the wind. *Don't* steer directly for the mark, for you would sail a much greater distance than necessary. As the diagram shows, you would actually travel a circular course *over the bottom* in order to arrive at the mark, B. If you steered high of the mark, as in AC, the current would set you down to it just about right.

Racing

Never start a race without first checking the tide tables, to determine the direction the tidal currents will be flowing during the race. If current tables cover the area in which you are racing, you'll have a clear picture of the direction for every hour. Otherwise, you'll have to depend on local knowledge, which you'll only acquire with experience. Local sailors who have sailed in your area over a period of years should be consulted, and with their help, plus your own determined observation, you should soon learn to use the currents to advantage.

Currents often flow at different velocities and in different directions at different parts of a race course. They may be accelerated and "bent" around headlands, for instance, or they may flow more rapidly in deep channels than over shallow flats. You must make every effort to figure out how currents will affect your course, and plot your tactics accordingly. Current charts are available in some areas, but it is better to know by experience and observation how the currents flow at different stages of the tide in different places in your racing area. In general, you will want to sail into areas of swift current when it will get you closer to the next mark and avoid these areas when they will take you away from the mark. You will also need to plan ahead. Perhaps it will be advantageous to sail through an area of swift current and do it as quickly as possible in order to get to an area of current (or wind) that will give you an ultimately greater advantage.

Note in the diagram how the current sets the boat from point A to point B on a beat to windward. Because of wind shifts, possible variables in the current, and other considerations, this is probably the fastest course to the mark. If current was the only consideration, and if it was constant, a starboard tack first leg would be just as fast. Some people think that the port tack leg is favored, but both boats will be exposed to the same current for the same length of time. Therefore, their speed and distance to the mark will be the same—discounting other variables.

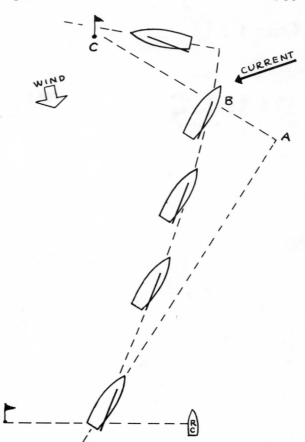

Chapter 16

RULES OF THE ROAD

The right-of-way rules governing the operation of water craft are of three classes: International Rules, set up by conferences of maritime nations: Inland Rules, devised by various Acts of Congress; and the Great Lakes Rules, which are "local," and apply only to the Great Lakes. These rules differ mainly in the signals and lights to be displayed by small craft. It is not necessary here to discuss all the applications and technicalities, since we are concerned primarily with the small sailboat without auxiliary power.

The rules have but one purpose—control of traffic on the water where risk of collision is involved by vessels meeting or crossing. While the rules apply primarily to powered craft, they distinguish between power and sail, and recognize that wind-driven craft cannot be maneuvered or controlled as easily as powered craft.

Therefore, Rule 20 states: "When a powered vessel and a sailing vessel are proceeding in a direction that involves risk of collision, the powered vessel shall keep out of the way of the sailing vessel." However, "This rule shall not give to a sailing vessel the right to hamper, in a narrow channel, the safe passage of a steam vessel which can navigate only inside that channel."

The International Rules state: "In obeying and construing these rules, any action taken should be positive, in ample time, and with due regard to the observance of good seamanship." Just because you have right-of-way, you are not relieved of responsibility to take any action to avoid collision. Therefore, regardless of the rules, it is good seamanship for the skipper of a small sailboat to give way to any craft that is considerably larger.

The International Rules governing sailing craft are incorporated in the *Racing Rules,* as defined in our chapter on racing. They are as follows:

1. A vessel which is on the port tack shall keep out of the way of a vessel which is on the starboard tack.
2. When both are running free, with the wind on different sides, the vessel which has the wind on the port side shall keep out of the way of the other.
3. When both are running free, the vessel which is to windward shall keep out of the way of the vessel which is to leeward.

Finally, notwithstanding anything contained in the above rules, every vessel *overtaking* any other shall keep out of the way of the *overtaken* vessel.

The foregoing rules are designated as *Steering Rules*. There are other rules governing lights, fog signals, and whistle signals. All sailboats must display running lights in accordance with applicable rules. Also the small sailboat under way at night is advised to leave on board a portable lantern or flashlight. Flashing a light on your sails at the approach of another vessel, reveals your position and approximate course or heading.

There is not room here to list all rules and regulations governing lights and signals as laid down by the Coast Guard, but you should study and memorize them. All are contained in various Coast Guard pamphlets, obtainable free of charge from any Coast Guard office. You should familiarize yourself with all rules applicable to *other craft,* so that you can identify them, and read their intentions from the signals they give, either by display of lights or sounds.

If you are going to do much night sailing, you must know the meaning of light combinations, so that you can reach a sound estimation of a situation immediately, *without reference to a book or a diagram*.

Chapter 17

CHARTS AND HOW TO USE THEM

The navigational chart has been described as the road map of the sea, the navigator's bible, and the sailor's guide to salvation from the perils of rocks and shoals. If you understand charts and how to use them, you can navigate anywhere, anytime. If you don't, you cannot navigate safely, at any time.

The charts you will be using are published by the National Oceanic and Atmospheric Administration of the U. S. Department of Commerce, and issued by the Coast Guard. You can purchase them from most marine supply stores, boatyards, and marinas.

Charts fall into four categories: *General Sailing Charts,* which are small-scale, for offshore navigation; *Coastal Charts,* for inshore navigation, for entering bays and harbors, and for large inland waterways, and *Harbor Charts,* for harbors, anchorage areas, and smaller inland waterways. There is also a series of *Small Craft Charts* covering harbors and waterways which are arranged in "strip" form. The last three are the ones you will most likely be using.

The scale of these charts will vary—the larger the scale the more detail will be shown. Harbor charts are on a scale larger than 1:50,000. The others, from 1:50,000 to 1:600,000.

What the Charts Show

Let's take a look at a chart and see what you can expect to find. Right under the title you'll find the *scale,* and a note telling whether the soundings (or depths at mean low water) are in *feet* or *fathoms.* A fathom equals six feet, so the number 5 on a chart could mean five feet depth or thirty feet, an important difference.

At the lower right edge of the chart you will find its number, and its price, which will be from fifty cents to a couple of dollars. You order a chart by its number, which corresponds to the Coast and Geodetic Survey catalogue of charts.

On all charts you will find one or more *compass roses.* You always use the compass rose nearest your position. You will see that the *outer* circle of the compass rose relates to *true north,* and the *inner* circle to *magnetic north.* In the center of the rose is printed the *variation,* and its increase or decrease annually, which will be explained later.

Charts also show what abbreviations

Preparing your charts is vital to successful navigation. (Photo by Dave Henderson)

are used. Familiarity with all abbreviations and symbols employed is of the utmost importance. They are all shown in color in *Chart #1,* priced at twenty-five cents. By all means see that you get a copy.

Prominent landmarks, such as towers, tanks, buildings, are shown as a circle with a dot in the center, and the name of the object alongside. To take accurate bearings from these, use the *dot*.

Navigational lights are designated by a red spot with a black dot in the center, and the characteristic of the light is named close by. "FL R 2½ sec 30ft 7M" means a flashing red light, flashing every 2½ seconds, 30 feet above mean high water, and visible 7 miles.

Buoys are shown as diamond shapes placed near a dot. They may be colored red or black, or striped. If the buoy is lighted, and has a whistle, bell, or gong, the fact is so indicated.

A buoy serves in a number of ways. Besides marking the course of a channel, it may locate submerged obstructions, such as a wreck, rocks, or the limit of a shoal. Although buoys are of various shapes and sizes, their *color* is the principal indication of their purpose.

You'll be using channel buoys more frequently than others. The rule of color is that red buoys mark the *right* side of the channel *when you are entering from seaward,* and the black mark the *left* side. An old reminder is "red-right-returning." In *leaving* port, the order is reversed— *black to starboard* and *red to port*. Channel buoys are numbered—red buoys always have *even* numbers, and black ones *odd* numbers. The number of each buoy will be found alongside it on the chart.

For night navigation, red buoys have *red* lights, and black buoys have *green* lights.

As to shape, red buoys are conical, and called *nuns*. Black buoys are cylindrical, like an oil drum set on end, and are called *cans*. A buoy with black and white vertical stripes marks the *middle* of a channel, and may be passed on either side. Black and red horizontal stripes indicate an obstruction and should be passed on the side indicated by the shape and top color of the buoy.

Let's go back and take another look at the compass rose on the chart, and take up the matter of variation. A compass does not point to the true North Pole but to the *magnetic* North Pole. These poles are quite a distance from each other, and the angle between them, *from where you are,* is called *variation*. It is so called because this angle varies from one area to another, and changes slightly with time.

I have before me an old chart. Within the compass rose is printed the following: "VAR 11°W (1954)—ANNUAL DE-CREASE 1'." This means that in 1954, from that particular area, the magnetic pole lay 11 degrees west of the true North Pole, and that this variation decreased one minute yearly.

In actual practice, the small-boat sailor need not be too concerned about variation. Courses are plotted on the chart from the magnetic pole. However, since the variation may increase or decrease from year to year, magnetic bearings may also change. Therefore, be sure your charts are *up to date*. Also, markers and light characteristics change occasionally. Using a chart that is three years old could conceivably lead you into trouble.

Chapter 18

THE COMPASS

The two indispensable tools of navigation are the chart and the compass, and neither is of much use without the other. It is not possible to give a course in navigation within these pages. All that can be done is to introduce these tools and explain their principal characteristics and how they can be put to work. There are a number of books on navigation, designed expressly for the small-boat skipper, and from them you can obtain all the help you may require for your specific needs.

Theoretically the needle of a magnetic compass points unerringly to the magnetic North Pole. But the compass in your boat will have errors, and the amount of error will vary with the boat's heading. These errors are caused by outside influences, primarily ferrous metals nearby, such as the motor in an auxiliary, iron fastenings in the boat itself, *or a beer can,* if it's close enough.

Deviation is the name given to these errors. In order to navigate you must know the deviation of your compass *on every heading,* and this is determined by reference to a *deviation card,* which you must make up yourself.

The compass has a line marked on the ring surrounding the compass card called the *lubber line,* which indicates the *heading of the boat.* The compass must be installed so that the line passing through the lubber line and the center of the card coincides with the centerline of the boat. The ideal position for the compass on a small boat is directly under or slightly ahead of the tiller, so it can be easily read by the helmsman.

Before we get into the methods of making a deviation card, it is imperative that you check the location of all iron or steel objects that are within five feet of your compass and make a mental note that they must always be stowed in the same place. As an example, suppose you normally stow a galvanized iron bucket in a cockpit locker on the port side about three feet from the compass. Once you have made your deviation card, you cannot change your mind and put it in the starboard locker. The magnetic pull on the compass needle will throw your deviation card out. Be ever alert, and keep loose metal objects away from the compass. A large screwdriver or wrench inadvertently left on the seat close by can make the needle wander.

The deviation card has an inner rose and an outer rose. The outer one represents *magnetic* direction, hereafter referred to as *magnetic course,* which you obtain from

MAGNETIC COURSE
TAKEN FROM CHART
ON OUTER ROSE

COMPASS COURSE
TO STEER BY
ON INNER ROSE

the chart. The inner rose represents your *boat's compass.*

Let us suppose that the course between two buoys shown on the chart is in a general east-west direction. You draw a straight line between them. With a protractor or parallel rules, you read the direction of this course from the *inner,* or *magnetic* rose on the chart. This happens to be 80 degrees heading east, and therefore 260 degrees heading west.

So you steer eastward, line up the two buoys by eye, and aim your boat directly along the line. You glance at the compass, and find that you are steering 85 degrees. You know that the course is actually 80,

for you have already plotted it on your chart. That 5-degree difference is the deviation of your compass *on that particular heading,* and it will always be there unless you move iron or steel objects into the vicinity of your compass.

On your deviation card, draw a line from the 80-degree mark on the *outer* rose to the 85-degree mark on the inner rose. Thus, you now have visible evidence of deviation, and if at any time the chart calls for a course of 80 degrees, follow the pencil line on the card, and you find you must steer 85 degrees. To complete the deviation card you must get a lot more pencil lines all around the rim of the rose.

Now reverse your course, from buoy to buoy. You know the magnetic course is 260 degrees, but your compass reads 256 degrees. So on this heading your deviation is 4 degrees. Draw a line on the card from 260 on the outer rose to 256 on the inner rose.

For purposes of illustration, I have drawn a simplified chart of a fictitious location. It shows various magnetic courses that can be used to obtain deviation on numerous headings—a tank and a flagpole on the northern shore, a lighthouse and a jetty beacon on the southern shore. Courses can be run between each and the channel buoys, and the same courses run *in reverse,* which doubles the number of checks for deviation that can be made.

The deviation card shown here illustrates how the various readings are entered. Notice that on the course between the tank and buoy *A,* the *magnetic* course and the *compass* course are identical. There is no deviation on this course, whether heading northerly or southerly.

The more readings you can obtain, the more accurate and useful your deviation card will be. If a magnetic course from the chart happens to fall *between* two lines on the deviation card, simply draw a line from the outer rose to the inner rose, approximating the lines on either side.

A compass is of no value unless you have confidence in it. To have that confidence, you must know its deviation with certainty, and *trust your knowledge of it.* It is not enough to make up a deviation card—you must make it a habit to check it constantly. Wherever you sail, lay out your magnetic course on the chart, and take every opportunity to check your deviation. Many disasters have occurred because the skipper thought he knew more than his compass.

There's one sure way to get in the habit of sailing by compass. Whenever you buy a new chart, spend an hour or so plotting magnetic courses, as described above. Draw a pencil line from buoy to buoy, and landmarks ashore that are shown on the chart. Mark on each line the magnetic course in both directions. From the scale at the bottom of the chart, using your dividers, measure the distance in nautical miles between each pair of reference points, and *enter them on the chart.*

Every time you set out on a trip, refer to the chart. You can tell at a glance the proper heading for each course, and your deviation card tells what your compass should read. Better yet, write the *compass* course below the *magnetic* course on the chart. You then don't have to refer to the deviation card at all. By entering the *distances* of each course on the chart, and timing yourself, you get to know the speed of your boat under various conditions of wind and sea. Thus you will always have a pretty fair idea how long it will take you to get from here to there.

Besides the compass and the chart, there are other valuable tools for navigating: tide tables, current tables, and current charts. The tide tables give the times of high and low water (and height) for every day of the year, in all coastal areas. The current tables give the times when flood and ebb currents begin to flow, the times at which they attain their maximum strengths, and the velocities of the latter for every day of the year. Current charts are available for many, but not all, areas. They consist of twelve charts, one for each hour of flood and ebb tides. The many small arrows show the direction of the current at any time, and figures show the velocity of the current at each arrow.

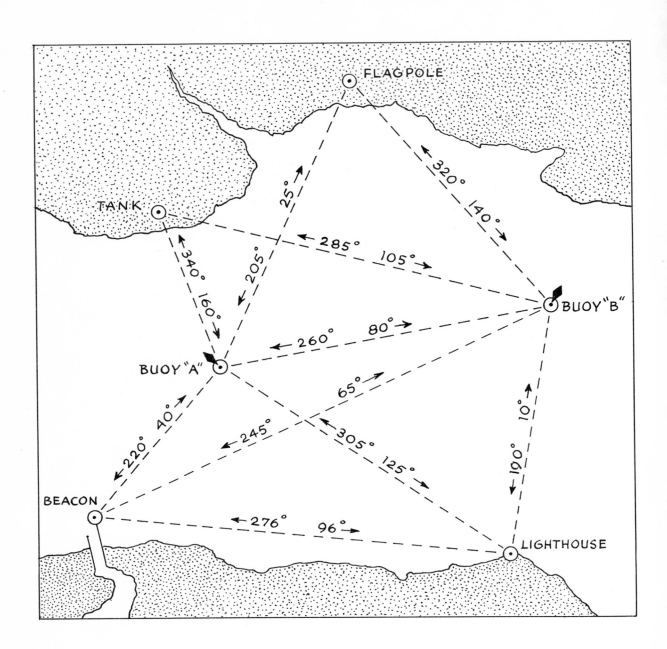

Chapter 19

PLANNING A CRUISE

Planning a cruise well in advance has several advantages. It can be done in leisure hours long before the sailing season starts, and it can make the difference between a pleasurable experience and an uncomfortable ordeal. Last-minute planning is invariably haphazard.

In deciding where you want to go, don't be too ambitious. There is no enjoyable relaxation if you have to keep pushing every minute. About twenty-five miles is the limit for a comfortable day's sail in a small boat. Experienced sailors will assure you that an early start is an important element of good planning, for both the beginning and the end of your day's adventure. The finest weather of the day is in the first couple of hours after sunrise. At the other end, getting your anchor down by half-past three or four o'clock in the afternoon gives you time to loaf, enjoy the surrounding scenery, or explore ashore before dinnertime. Trying to find an anchorage in a strange harbor after sundown, when you are weary, hungry, and irritable, is not very enjoyable.

Having decided where you want to go, study your chart carefully. Your compass courses are laid out, and landmarks are noted. Examine the coastline, and note the *soundings*. Look for a sheltered cove where you can duck in if you run into bad weather. Refer to the tide and current tables for that day. You'll want to know whether the current will be helping you or working against you, and whether you'll be anchoring on a rising or falling tide.

Keep a log of your cruise. This can be a simple notebook, in which you write the time of your departure, wind direction and force, the time of passing important buoys or landmarks, shifts of wind force or direction, time of arrival, and expenses. This log will help you to relive the cruise some winter evening and will be a valuable reference when planning another cruise. Finally, be *forehanded,* and plan not only for the expected, but for the unexpected.

Chapter 20

MARLINSPIKE SEAMANSHIP

Familiarity with the use of rope—the knots, bends, hitches, and splices, and their applications—is one of the basic elements of seamanship. The safety of your boat can depend on your knowledge of these skills, and the sooner you master them, the better.

Before putting rope to work, it is necessary to understand its anatomy—the parts of its structure, the way it is put together, and why. Although materials and techniques have been improved, its construction is the same as it was two thousand years ago—fibers twisted together into yarns, yarns twisted into strands, and the strands laid up into rope. Most of the rope you'll be using will have three strands, as in the illustration, twisted together right-handed, and is termed *right-laid*. If you were to coil this rope counterclockwise, or left-handed, it would come off the coil in kinks and snarls. Therefore always coil rope clockwise, or *right-handed,* and it will run freely from the coil.

Types of Rope

MANILA

Manila rope is made from the fibers of a plant grown in the Philippines called the "abaca." The natural fibers vary in length from three to ten or twelve feet, the shortest being used in the poorest quality of rope, the longest in first-grade rope. Low-grade rope is rough and hairy, hard on the hands and low in strength. "Yacht rope," the finest grade of manila, is smooth and slick, easy on the hands, the strongest, and the highest in price. When wet, manila gains in strength, and at the same time, shrinks considerably.

One bad feature of manila is its low resistance to rot. Rot is caused by a fungus that thrives on dampness plus heat. Manila rope should be kept as dry as possible, well aired, and out of the direct sun. Stowing a coil of rope away below deck when it is wet is the best way to promote rot. There are a number of preservatives on the market today for treating rope, which reduce its tendency to rot and greatly prolong its useful life.

NYLON

Synthetic fibers, with their superior qualities, have almost pushed the natural fibers, such as manila, out of the picture, as far as rope for sailing craft is concerned. The initial cost is higher, but the incomparable performance of synthetic rope far outweighs the price factor.

Nylon rope has two superior characteristics—an almost unbelievable elasticity (almost 30 percent) and great strength. The breaking strength of ½-inch manila is 2,650 pounds; the breaking strength of ½-inch nylon, *6,250* pounds. Thus a large coil of nylon anchor line is lighter and less bulky than a manila line of the same length.

Its ability to stretch and recover like a resilient spring makes nylon admirably suited for anchor and mooring lines, and for dock and towing lines. On the other hand, its great elasticity makes it entirely unsuitable for running rigging, that is, sheets and halyards. It is also very slick and slippery, which, in the smaller sizes, makes it hard to hold on to.

The nylon fiber is waterproof and rotproof, and therefore has a very long life. Its only apparent enemy is sunlight. A coil of nylon line left in the broiling sun for a long period will deteriorate and, like most synthetics, will melt if heat is applied.

DACRON

Dacron rope is used principally for sheets and halyards, since it has low elasticity. It is soft, pliable, easy to hold, and easy on the hands. Its strength is somewhat higher than manila, and less than nylon. Because of its whiteness and soft finish, it resembles cotton in appearance.

In addition to 3-strand rope, there is also braided Dacron. It has no superior for sheets, since it never kinks, and with its smooth, woven surface, it reeves through a block or fairlead with a minimum amount of friction. If you want the best, braided Dacron is it.

POLYPROPYLENE

This is used mainly in the commercial fishing industry for various components of fishnets and other gear. The reason for its inclusion here is that yachtsmen have discovered it to be an excellent rope for dock lines.

It is extremely light in weight, has high elasticity, and will float if dropped overboard. It has the look and feel of manila, and is easily spliced. A knot, hitch, or bend will not jam up tightly, as in manila, and therefore can be easily undone. When securing to a cleat or bitt, therefore, take an extra turn or hitch to prevent its loosening.

COTTON

The use of cotton is restricted to what is called "small stuff," flag halyards, lanyards, and lashings. Cotton rope, when wet, becomes stiff as wire, and a knot or hitch is almost impossible to remove. Like manila, cotton rope has largely been supplanted by nylon and Dacron.

Knot, Bend, or Hitch?

In the eyes of the landlubber, any time you use rope to secure or fasten anything, you "tie a knot." But once aboard a boat he'll discover that a seaman variously employs knots, bends, hitches, and splices, each having specific applications.

There are several kinds of knot: those used to bind something together, or to secure a package, such as the *reef knot;* those used to form a temporary loop such as the *bowline;* the *knob knot,* where a knob is formed in a rope end to provide a handhold; the *stopper knot* to prevent it from unreeving.

A *hitch* is used to make a rope fast to *another object.*

A *bend* joins *two rope ends* to *each other.*

A *lashing* secures one object to another.

A *seizing* binds ropes together or to other objects, more or less permanently.

A *stopping* serves the same purpose, but only temporarily.

A *whipping* is a binding of small-stuff placed about a rope end to prevent its unlaying or fraying.

Knots

REEF KNOT

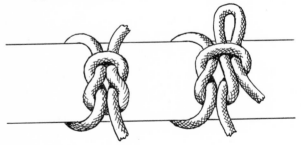

REEF KNOT   SLIPPED REEF KNOT

Often called the *square,* or *sailor's knot,* the reef knot is probably the most universally known and remembered of all knots. At sea, it is used in reefing sails or lashings and seizings, and for these alone it is excellent. But *under no circumstances should it ever be used as a bend,* to tie two ropes together! If the two ropes are of unequal size, or one is stiffer than the other, the knot is almost certain to slip when under a load.

All knots, bends, and hitches tighten up and are difficult to untie when they are wet or under a strain, and the reef knot is the worst of all. Therefore, the sailor can modify it into the *slipped reef knot.* If you grasp the free end and jerk it across the knot, it will instantly capsize into a pair of reversed half-hitches, which can be stripped off with one hand.

BOWLINE

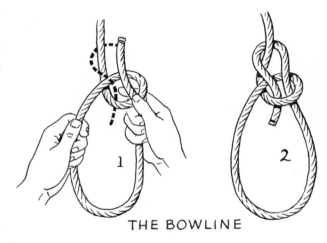

THE BOWLINE

The most useful of all sailor's knots is the bowline. Used to put a loop in a rope end, it can be tied easily in an instant, will never slip, and can be untied readily even when soaking wet.

STOPPER, OR FIGURE-EIGHT KNOT

Sometimes a sheet will inadvertently get away from you and run out through the blocks. To prevent this accidental unreeving, always tie a stopper knot in each sheet-end. It is easy to tie and untie.

THE FIGURE-EIGHT KNOT

Hitches

CLOVE

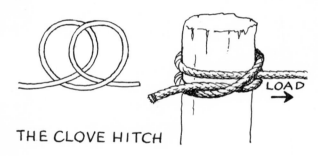

THE CLOVE HITCH

There are many different hitches that may be used to make a rope fast to a variety of objects—a pile, bitt, spar, ring, or hook. The clove hitch is the most commonly used, quickest to tie, and easiest to remember. It consists of two single hitches, one superimposed on the other, and is most useful for securing to a post or rail where the pull will be *at an angle.* Hence its common use in dock lines, as a temporary mooring.

The clove hitch must never be regarded as really *secure,* but as a utility hitch for *temporary* use. There is an unpredictable amount of initial slip when a strain is put on it, and it will loosen or slip if subjected to intermittent pulls in *different directions.* On a *square* post it is most unsafe. Always remember to set it up snugly by hand before putting a strain on it, and never use it where great strength and safety are imperative.

ROLLING

This is the hitch to use in securing a rope to a spar for a *lengthwise pull.* Its great virtue is its ability to hold without any danger of slipping when tied on a highly polished surface. When you are stepping or unshipping a mast, it secures the sling to which the tackle is hooked. When aloft in a bosun's chair, secure your lifeline to the mast with a rolling hitch, for it will not slip if your weight falls on it suddenly. To secure a light line to a wire shroud, this is the hitch to use.

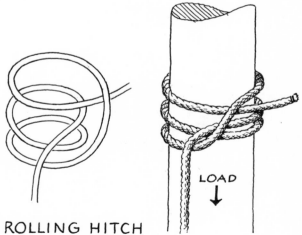

ROLLING HITCH

Note in the illustration, that no fewer than two round turns are taken to the right about the spar, *below* the standing part, and the working end is then brought up over all and finished off with two single hitches to the right. Always set the hitches up snugly before putting a strain on the rope.

riodically and retied to bring the wear on a fresh part of the rope.

Bends

DOUBLE SHEET

This is a general-utility bend, used to unite two rope ends as in lengthening an anchor line, to secure a line to a loop, or to connect a small line to the end of a much larger rope. It is very strong, and can be easily untied when wet. As in all bends and hitches, it should be set up taut by hand before applying a load.

FISHERMAN'S BEND

DOUBLE SHEET BEND

FISHERMAN'S

To *bend* your anchor line to the ring or shackle of your anchor, the fisherman's bend is the strongest and safest. To the purist, it is actually a *hitch*, but sailors called it a bend for years, so a bend it must be.

Note that *two* parts of the rope pass through the ring, which gives maximum bearing surface, and reduces the amount of wear and chafe. But because there is wear and chafe, it should be inspected pe-

In learning all the foregoing applications, the rope is considered to have three parts—the *working end*, which is the extremity being manipulated, the *standing part*, which is the inactive part, and the *bight*, which might be described as an arc or curve in the rope no smaller than a semicircle (if smaller, it would be a loop) or any central segment of the rope between the ends.

A true seaman is able to construct any of the rope tricks instantly, and in total darkness. The only way to achieve proficiency is to practice—over and over and over.

Splicing

There are many different kinds of splices for specific uses, but the average small-boat skipper generally needs but two—the *eye splice,* for forming a permanent loop, as in dock lines, and the *short splice,* which he'll need only infrequently, for adding one length of rope to another permanently.

The experienced sailor can splice small rope with his fingers alone, but the beginner should employ a fid or marlinspike to open the strands for tucking. Study the illustrations to learn how to open the rope with the fid, and the method of tucking the strands.

THE EYE SPLICE

For practice in making an eye splice, take a length of ⅜-inch *manila* rope. Synthetics are more difficult to handle, and with manila it is easier to learn to splice neatly. About six or eight inches from the end put on a tight seizing of twine or marline. Since it is only temporary, you can use common electrician's friction tape in place of twine. Unlay the rope carefully to the seizing, and put a similar seizing on the end of each strand to prevent them from unlaying.

Now bring the working end up to the right of the standing part to form an eye or loop. At the point where you wish to start the splice, open the rope to begin the tucks. Right here the beginner generally goes wrong. For the sake of clarity, the strands in the diagram are labeled *a, b,* and *c.* But the rope in your hands bears no labels, so try to think of the strands as the left-hand, the center, and the right-hand strands. All tucks are made *against the lay,* which means from right to left.

Referring to diagram #1, note that strand A is tucked under strand *a,* B is tucked under *b,* and C under *c.* Left under left, center under center, and right under right.

Always tuck the center strand first, the left-hand next, and the *right-hand last.* Diagram #2 shows the first tuck.

Diagram #3 shows the second tuck, with strand A going over *b* and under *a.* Now, in order to tuck the last strand, C, it is necessary to flop the whole works over, to get at it from the back. Diagram #4 shows how it will appear from the back.

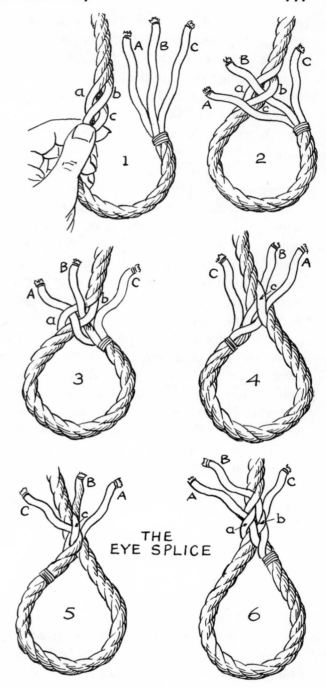

THE EYE SPLICE

Diagram #5 shows the last strand, C, tucked under *c, from right to left.* Now draw up each tucked strand snugly and evenly, and you are ready to start the second round of tucks.

It makes no difference which strand you start with. In diagram #6 it happens to be strand B, with which the splice was originally started. It passes over *a* and under the next strand to the *left*. Continue by tucking the other two strands, over one and under one, to the left. All three strands having been tucked twice, tuck each strand once more in sequence, and the splice is completed.

Now look it over and see whether it is a good or bad splice. It is absolutely imperative that each of the tucked strands be drawn up with equal tension, so each bears an equal share of the load. Note also that in drawing up a strand after tucking, *do not* pull it back toward the eye or loop, but forward, in a direction nearly parallel with the standing part.

If the splice looks fair and even, lay it down on the deck and roll it back and forth under your foot. This fairs up the splice, and evens up the tension of the strands. Under no circumstance should you cut the protruding strand ends off flush with the rope—leave at least a half inch of each strand showing.

So much for basic techniques. After you have made a few practice splices you should be able to dispense with the diagrams.

Splicing nylon and polypropylene requires different treatment. The strength of a splice is obtained mainly through friction, and these two materials are too slick and slippery to afford much friction. Therefore, while three tucks are sufficient for manila, five tucks should be taken when working with these synthetics. Furthermore, the protruding strand ends should be covered by a seizing of twine, or other material, to keep the ends from working back into and out of the splice. The best way to cover the ends neatly and securely is to wrap with black plastic electrician's tape or silver duct tape.

THE SHORT SPLICE

The short splice is used to join two ropes of *equal diameter*. It cannot be used in running rigging, since it doubles the diameter of the rope at the splice, and therefore will not reeve through a block or fairlead.

As in the eye splice, all tucks are made over one and under one against the lay, from right to left. You start as before: put a seizing on each rope about six inches from the end, and a temporary whipping on the end of each strand.

Clutch the two ropes together as in diagram #1, each strand of one rope between two of the other, and clap on a narrow, tight seizing where they join, as in diagram #2. The first two seizings can now be removed.

Since you have already mastered the eye splice, the strands are not labeled in the diagram. Each set of strands are tucked three times, in sequence. Starting with the strands on the left, make the first tuck as in diagram #3. Rotate the splice away from you and tuck the second strand, as shown in diagram #4. Tuck the third and last strand as in diagram #5.

Continue tucking in turn, the three strands a second and a third time, and the splice will be half finished. Now turn the rope and the splice around on your lap, bringing the remaining three strands on the left side. Take three tucks with each, as you did before, and the splice is completed. If you are still with us, it should look like diagram #6.

Whippings

Every rope end requires a whipping to prevent it from unlaying. Landlubbers tie a knot in the end, but to do this is senseless to a sailor, for the rope cannot be passed through an eye or block. Whippings are put on with either waxed sail twine or tarred Italian hemp marline, depending on the size of the rope. It is customary to use marline on rope that is ¾ inch in diameter or larger. When you are using sail twine, it is always *doubled,* and waxed with beeswax. While there are several dozen ways to whip a rope, the *sailmaker's* whipping shown here stays put, doesn't come apart, and is particularly handsome. Never put a whipping on close to the end of the rope; put it several inches inboard, and cut it off after it is finished.

The rope is unlaid carefully two or three inches. Then a loose loop of twine is placed over one strand, with the short, inactive end and the long working end brought out between the other two strands. Now lay up the three rope strands again, being careful to preserve their lay. The loop should be left several inches long.

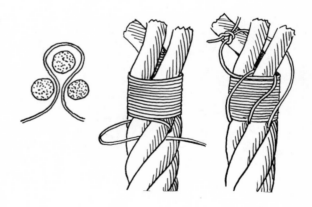

With the working end of the twine, put on the required number of turns tightly and evenly. Then bring the loop up over the top of *the strand it encircles*. Now pull hard on the inactive short end, which will draw the loop up tightly. Bring both ends up to the top and tie them tightly together with a reef knot. The excess rope should be cut off no closer than ⅜ inch from the end of the whipping. The *width* of a whipping should be no less than the diameter of the rope.

Coiling and Stowing Rope

A good seaman keeps his inactive ropes neatly coiled at all times—not for appearance, but because he has learned that the safe, efficient operation of his vessel depends on orderliness. He knows that a neat coil of rope is ready at all times for immediate use. Rope thrown on deck in a haphazard heap cannot be used until it is overhauled and the kinks and snarls are worked out. By that time, it may be too late.

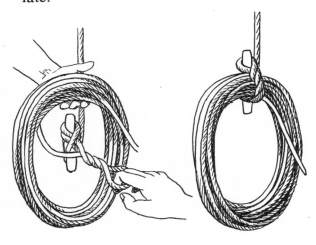

Once a sail is hoisted, the surplus halyard should be coiled immediately and hung on the cleat to which it is belayed, ready to be cast off in an instant. The illustration shows a proper halyard coil.

Never start the coil with the bitter end, for this will result in kinks. Start the turns of the coil next to the cleat, and when it is completed, leave the bitter end hanging a little below the coil. This helps prevent the end from becoming fouled in the turns.

With the coil in your left hand, reach through the coil with your right and pull the bight of the standing part through. Twist it several turns to the *left,* or against the lay, and slip it on the cleat. The coil

is secure, and the turns cannot possibly be disturbed. When you are ready to cast off the halyard, slip the bight off the cleat, and drop the coil on deck, *face down.* It is then ready to run, free and clear.

The next illustration shows a neat and handy way to make up a coil of spare rope for hanging below deck. After the rope has been coiled, make a bight near the end by doubling it. Take a hitch to the right about the head of the coil, then another hitch to the left. This resembles a clove hitch, which it isn't.

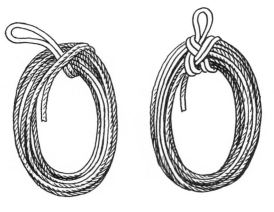

An anchor line, being too large to be coiled in the hand, is coiled down directly on the deck, clockwise, starting next to the anchor. Each turn should be a trifle larger than the preceding. Capsize the coil carefully, rearranging any turn that is out of line, and then put on four stops of marline or light line. Tie each with a slipped reef knot, for ease in casting off. Thus your line is made secure, ready for use without overhauling, and cannot become fouled.

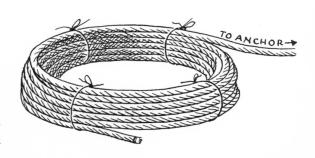

TO ANCHOR →

Chapter 21

WATER SAFETY

Keeping Ahead of Trouble

The best way to remedy trouble is to anticipate it. The dictionary defines anticipation as "the prevention of future evil, and the securing of future good, by timely looking forward, and acting upon what is foreseen." Old-time seamen called this action "forehanded."

This does not mean *excessive* caution, but it does mean a sensible understanding of the capabilities of your boat, and of yourself. As a beginner, you are venturing into a world where a whole new set of rules applies, and the sooner you learn the rules, the more quickly you achieve carefree enjoyment of the sport. Anyone who ventures forth upon the sea in small boats meets up with trouble sooner or later. Experience and knowledge of those related skills that comprise *seamanship* help you keep minor troubles from becoming serious ones.

Know Your Boat

The first rule is to *know your boat*. In selecting, buying, and learning to sail your boat you will have learned quite a bit about her, but that is not enough, for you must know she reacts in all conditions of wind and sea, what her limitations are, and what she *cannot* do with safety. You must learn how much wind she can handle under full sail, and recognize the point at which she begins to labor, and must be reefed.

The most important factor in sailing with safety is the *condition* of your boat. This demands eternal vigilance, constant inspection, and proper maintenance. A bent turnbuckle may indicate metal fatigue or partial fracture, and you should replace it immediately. The possible consequence of not doing so is dismasting when it lets go under strain. A minor leak ignored and unattended, can spread to serious proportions when the boat is wracked and strained in heavy seas, and result in swamping or worse. A chafed and frayed mooring line can part when you're not around, and the boat goes ashore, pounding herself to death on the rocks. These are but a few of the things that can happen for lack of "forehandedness."

A good seaman sees that his boat is "well-found." This means that she has everything aboard that is necessary for safe and efficient operation, not only un-

A capsized boat is easily righted and rescued when cool heads prevail. (Photos by John W. Nash)

der normal conditions, but in *emergencies.* He'll have a small ditty box, containing such things as spare shackles, a coil of wire for seizings, an assortment of nails and screws, some calking cotton, and an adequate assortment of tools—hammer, cutting pliers, adjustable wrench, and several screwdrivers—all kept well oiled and free of rust.

He'll have a ditty bag, in which he keeps his sewing kit—sewing palm, sail needles, assorted sail twine and beeswax for sail repairs, a ball of marline, and a good sailor's sheath knife. He'll have several coils of *new* rope of the proper size for replacement of sheets, halyards, or spring lines, small lanyards or light lines for lashings, and an odd piece of canvas for chafing gear. Unless his boat is a very small one, he'll have a spare anchor and cable stowed up in the forepeak, his insurance against the "big blow" he may some day be caught in.

An adequate bilge pump *that works,* and a good compass should be on the boat at all times; also an up-to-date chart of the waters in which you'll be sailing. Equally important, you should constantly *practice* sailing by compass course and chart. If you are planning to sail to a point only four miles away and in plain sight, lay out the course on the chart, plot the compass course in degrees, and steer for the spot *by compass*. Once you are accustomed to sailing in this manner, you'll be prepared for the day when a pea-soup fog rolls in and blots out all the familiar landmarks. This is your "forehandedness" again— learning a skill while you *don't* need it, against the day when you *must have it*.

Life Jackets

It used to be considered "chicken" to have to wear a life jacket (the U. S. Coast Guard prefers to call life jackets "personal flotation devices"), but the experienced sailor knows that they are, indeed, very important devices, to be put on without hesitation when they might be needed. The Coast Guard now approves several classes of PFDs, including specially designed sailor's vests, developed by the North American Yacht Racing Union, that can be worn by an active crew member. The older types of life jackets approved by the Coast Guard were designed to be worn by *passengers* in commercial vessels who took no part in the working of the vessel. These vests, which are designed for maximum effectiveness, to float an unconscious person face up, are too restrictive to be worn by someone engaged in handling a sailboat.

Many racing sailors wear these newer vests as a matter of course, and they set a good example for other sailors to follow. A life jacket, vest, or PFD will do you no good if it is in the locker. Now that there are comfortable and effective PFDs available, you no longer have an excuse for

Life jacket of urethane-coated nylon, in high-visibility gold. (Photo by courtesy of Stearns Manufacturing Company)

not wearing one whenever the wind is strong or the water is either rough or cold.

Watch the Weather

Another important element in sailing with safety is learning to be weather-wise. Weather is the greatest single factor affecting the pleasure you get in sailing. It determines whether you are going to have a smooth, enjoyable trip, or a rough, uncomfortable, or even dangerous one. But your greatest interest in weather is in the possible changes that may occur between the time you set out and the time you return. At its worst, it can affect the safety of your boat and your life. Therefore, it is important that you learn some of the fundamental principles that govern the weather, and become continually observant of the "signs and portents."

It is not necessary that you take a course in meteorology, but you should learn to use the many aids that are constantly available to you. Weather bureau reports and forecasts for your area can be heard hourly by radio, your morning or evening newspaper carries the weather maps, a good barometer foretells changes twelve hours in advance, and the clouds in the sky around you are visible signs of what is happening.

A good barometer is an essential aid. It measures the pressure of the atmosphere, and by observing the rise and fall of pressure you can reasonably predict weather changes. A falling barometer, accompanied by rising temperature, generally means bad weather—rain, and southerly winds, increasing. A rising barometer means a clear-up, and fair weather, with winds in the northern sector.

One common threat to the small-boat sailor's peace of mind is the sudden squall or thunderstorm. Very common during the summer months, the thunderstorm materializes very suddenly, generally in late afternoon. This type of storm is of short duration, and high seas do not have time to build up to any great extent. The main concern is the wind, which can be violent and dangerous.

Your first warning is a darkening sky, generally in the northwest, and the appearance of a *thunderhead*, a massive vertical cloud formation, with sharply defined edges, and an anvil top, which may not

be visible. This cloud formation, called *cumulo-nimbus,* is easily recognized.

From the time the thunderhead makes up until the first big blast of wind hits, there is seldom more than one half to three quarters of an hour in which to prepare for it. If you are close to shore, get in as quickly as possible. If you can't reach shore in time, get the sails down right away, and if the water is shoal enough, anchor until it is over. With the first gust there is a drop in temperature, and as the wind eases off, rain follows. Within an hour, it is generally all over.

Cumulus clouds are indicative of fair weather. They have soft, rounded edges,

are bright and "cottony," and near the horizon they have flat undersides. As long as they are up there, there will be no appreciable change in the weather.

Cirrus clouds are likely to foretell a change, usually for the worse. They bunch together, wispy in appearance. A sky so clouded is called "mackerel," because of its resemblance to the mackerel's markings.

Earlier, I mentioned the importance of knowing your boat's limitations. As the force of the wind steadily increases, there comes a time when the boat can no longer carry full sail, and is overpowered. It heels far over, spilling wind from the sails, and becomes increasingly difficult to handle; forward speed is reduced to a minimum. Sailing in this situation is uncomfortable, senseless, and dangerous, since it can ultimately lead to swamping and capsizing. The alternative is shortening sail by reefing *before it becomes imperative.*

The inexperienced beginner invariably fails to see the signs of worsening weather and carries on too long. How strong a wind it is safe to sail in depends on the size of your boat. A 30-knot wind is no

threat to a 60-footer, but for a small centerboarder under 25 feet, it is a *near gale.* Learn to read the signs all about you.

Whitecaps appear only occasionally when the wind force is 11 to 16 knots, which is considered a *moderate breeze* . . . fine sailing for small boats. As the wind increases to a *fresh breeze,* 17 to 21 knots, the water is pretty well covered with whitecaps, and the waves noticeably increase in length. A boat under 25 feet can safely sail in a fresh breeze without reefing, but she will be sailing at maximum speed, and the going will be rough and wet, particularly if she is close-hauled. Now, *if* you are within a half-hour's sail of your mooring, or a sheltered cove, and *if* the wind does not increase in force, you'll be all right.

But suppose the wind shows no sign of abating, is steadily getting stronger, and you are a long way from shelter. *Now* is the time to anchor and take in a reef, while the boat is manageable. Under shortened sail, the boat will foot faster, be on a more normal angle of heel, ship less water, and handle more easily and comfortably.

Remember the old adage—the good seaman weathers the storm he cannot avoid, and avoids the storm he cannot weather. Every sailor sooner or later runs into heavy weather, but you *don't have to* leave the safety of a snug mooring and go out in the face of bad weather. Get a late weather report, check your barometer, scan the outside waters for whitecaps and high seas, and if there are other boats out sailing, notice how they are acting and if any are reefed. Then, if you have any doubts about going out, *stay where you are*—accept a change of plans and disappointment, and avoid trouble.

Capsizing

Nearly all small-boat sailors experience capsizing at least once in their careers, and if they haven't—*they should*. It is standard practice in all junior sailing classes for the instructor to demonstrate capsizing to the youngsters early in their training. The purpose is not to teach them *how* to capsize, but what to do *when* they capsize. They learn right at the beginning that center-board boats do not sink and will support many people in the water; that there is a proper routine to follow before and after help arrives. These cardinal rules should be indelibly fixed in your mind:

1. Immediately upon capsizing, look for your crew and make sure he (or they) is all right. Sometimes a crew member, sitting to leeward, is caught under the sail as the boat goes over.

2. Put on life jackets (you should already have them on in heavy weather); the jacket keeps you warm, conserves your energy for the necessary exertions, and holds you up when you become tired.

3. *Stay with the boat.* Boats are always found after capsizing, but people are not always found. *Don't* swim away to rescue your two-dollar seat cushion or your favorite yachting cap. If you cannot right and bail your boat without assistance, hang on and wait for rescue. There are invariably other boats nearby. If you are at sea, and it looks as though you may have a long wait, tie yourself and crew together with any available piece of line. Again, I repeat, *stay with the boat:* it won't sink, and once you swim away from

its safety, you may not be able to get back.

When the rescue boat arrives, request that it stay clear until you get the boat ready for towing. Cut or untie the halyards, and get the sails off. Jam the sails under the deck, if possible, or tie a line around them by which they can be hauled aboard the rescue craft. Secure a towline with a bowline knot around the *mast,* not the deck cleat. With the centerboard down, you should be able to climb on it and right the boat, holding on to the topside or rail, and using your weight as a lever. You are now ready to be towed, and here the fun starts.

Invariably the skipper of the rescue boat has had no experience whatsoever in towing a swamped sailboat, and invariably he tows *too fast.* Many a sailor has waved off a well-meaning rescuer, preferring to allow the capsized boat to drift ashore rather than see her seriously damaged by inept boat-handling. Plead earnestly with your rescuer, therefore, to *please* go dead slow. The tow may no sooner start than your boat slowly turns over on her side again. You cannot tow a sailboat with her mast in the water without damaging her. If the boat starts to turn over, ask the towing boat to stop immediately.

It is very difficult to keep the boat upright while being towed, since she has no buoyancy while full of water. Your best bet is to haul yourself halfway up on the stern, in dead center, where you can apply a certain amount of leverage when she starts to roll one way or the other.

Instead of towing into a dock, it is better to go into shoal water off a sandy beach, where you drop the towline. Here you can work the boat into the beach and bail out more conveniently.

Chapter 22

COURTESY AFLOAT

The dictionary defines courtesy as "genuine and habitual politeness." But the courtesy expected of those who go to sea for pleasure embraces more. It is the acceptance of customary ways of doing things, observance of the traditions and customs of a gentlemanly sport, and adherence to its highest standards. Finally, it implies recognition of the rights and privileges of your fellow seamen.

Flags

In boating there is a factor that is steeped in tradition: a boat can fly a flag —the yacht ensign, the burgee of the yacht club to which the owner belongs, and the owner's distinctive private signal. Flown where all can see it, the flag automatically obliges the owner to handle his boat and conduct himself in a manner that reflects credit on every organization or group of which he is a member.

The display of flags on a small sailboat is rather limited, but you should fly them *correctly*.

The yacht ensign is flown on a staff at the stern when the boat is at anchor. It is displayed at 0800 and is taken in at sundown. When the boat is under way, it may be flown at the peak on a gaff-rigged boat, or from the leach of a jib-headed mainsail, a third of the way down from the headboard, or on the stern staff if the boom does not overhang the stern.

Racing yachts do not fly an ensign but signify that they have finished or withdrawn from a race by flying their ensign.

On a single-masted boat, the owner's private signal is flown at the masthead only when the boat is under way. Upon the boat's coming to anchor, the private signal is hauled down and the burgee of the owner's club goes to the masthead.

If your boat is a yawl, ketch, or schooner, the club burgee is flown at the head of the forward mast, and the private signal at the head of the aftermast.

These are the *only* flags the small-boat owner need concern himself with, and they should be flown correctly or not at all.

Tying flags haphazardly on the shrouds, stays, or elsewhere is an indication to all observers of sloppiness and disrespect, no different from washing your car with the national colors. Proper observance of flag etiquette reveals the owner's pride and respect for the customs and traditions of the sport.

The Rights of Others

Those who sail for pleasure all share the same enjoyment, the same disappointments, and the same hazards and troubles.

The forces of wind and sea make no distinction between rich and poor. All sailors have equal rights and privileges, and the majority respect the other fellow's share in them.

Unfortunately, there is always a small minority whose code of conduct is based on an attitude of "do as you please, and to the devil with everyone else." No book will change their attitude in the slightest degree.

But to the earnest beginner who is anxious to start off on the right tack, I can offer some helpful advice. One major source of ill feeling lies in the rules of the road and their application. A small boat can be maneuvered more quickly and easily than a large one. It also requires less room for maneuvering.

Supposing you are sailing down a narrow channel before the wind in your 19-foot day sailer. Glancing astern you discover you are being rapidly overtaken by a 50-foot yawl. Now, under the rules of the road, you have the right-of-way, and the yawl, being the overtaking vessel, must keep clear. Technically and legally you have the right to maintain your course. But *morally,* the right thing to do is to ease over to windward a bit and give him plenty of room to pass. "Do unto others as you would have them do unto you."

Another important thought is to *keep clear of boats that are racing.* Stay outside their racing course if at all possible. If there is no alternative but to sail through them, give everyone else the right-of-way, and do everything in your power to avoid interfering. Cross *astern* of a boat closehauled, rather than across his bow. Keep to *leeward* of a boat running free. Luff up, go about, or jibe rather than blanket a contestant and take his wind. You'll have lost nothing but a few minutes of free time, but you'll have gained the good

will of those who are trying to win what is to them an important race.

Rules of the road are as necessary to safety on the water as on the highway. They were designed to avoid collision and potential danger. But where no danger is involved, the small-boat sailor should not insist on his technical right-of-way. Put yourself in the other fellow's place and "give a little."

There's another matter in which you can maintain friendly relations with your fellow seamen. Don't be a seagoing litterbug. For some strange reason, people who neatly set their garbage at the curb for the Monday collection often have no compunction about tossing their garbage nonchalantly overboard when they are on the water.

This may be necessary if you are offshore, well out to sea. But in the tidal waters of a small harbor it is distinctly out of order, and in many areas, against the law. Keep your refuse in a heavy paper bag or bucket, and dispose of it in a proper place ashore.

Since time immemorial it has been the unwritten law of the sea that you go to the aid of a seaman in distress. Salvage rights and other legal aspects that are the concern of merchant vessels are not of particular interest to the owner of a 24-foot sailboat, for in small boating the hazards to persons, which cannot be measured in dollars and cents, usually override the hazards to property. But the *obligation* still holds.

The universal willingness of yachtsmen to give assistance to each other, often at considerable risk to themselves, is one of the bonds that unite them in a special fraternity. Keep an eye on the other fellow. If he appears to be in trouble, don't wait for a signal of distress—offer help. Tomorrow, *you* may be on the receiving end.